Debating Emerging Adulthood

Debating Emerging Adulthood

Adulthood

Stage or Process?

JEFFREY JENSEN ARNETT

MARION KLOEP

LEO B. HENDRY

JENNIFER L. TANNER

OXFORD

UNIVERSITY PRESS

2011

OXFORD

UNIVERSITY PRESS

Oxford University Press
Oxford University Press, Inc., publishes works that further
Oxford University's objective of excellence
in research, scholarship, and education.

Oxford New York
Auckland   Cape Town   Dar es Salaam   Hong Kong   Karachi
Kuala Lumpur   Madrid   Melbourne   Mexico City   Nairobi
New Delhi   Shanghai   Taipei   Toronto

With offices in
Argentina   Austria   Brazil   Chile   Czech Republic   France   Greece
Guatemala   Hungary   Italy   Japan   Poland   Portugal   Singapore
South Korea   Switzerland   Thailand   Turkey   Ukraine   Vietnam

Copyright © 2011 by Oxford University Press

Published by Oxford University Press, Inc.
198 Madison Avenue, New York, New York 10016
www.oup.com

Library of Congress Cataloging-in-Publication Data
Debating emerging adulthood : stage or process / [edited by] Jeffrey J. Arnett... [et al.].
  p. cm.
  1. Adulthood–Psychologial aspects. 2. Maturation (Psychology) I. Arnett, Jeffrey Jensen.
  BF724.5.D43 2011
305.242–dc22

                                                                        2010020139

ISBN: 978-0-19-975717-6

Contents

SECTION III: Rejoinders

Conclusion

Debating Emerging Adulthood

I

The Curtain Rises: A Brief Overview of the Book

Jeffrey Jensen Arnett, Leo B. Hendry, Marion Kloep, and Jennifer L. Tanner

Prologue

"All the world's a stage," begins a famous monologue from William Shakespeare's *As You Like It,* and when we go to the theatre to watch a play we are always struck by the way the stage is illuminated to enhance the actors' performances and heighten the emotions of the audience. Furthermore, we note how everything is focused on the stage.

But there are other ways of presenting a performance, and stories and plays sometimes train the spotlight on the players interacting with each other and perhaps confronting the audience members either by their words and actions or by moving among them—thereby eliminating the focus on the stage, and rather placing the emphasis on the behaviors of the participants—"All the men and women [are] players."

This book has similar, contrasting qualities. By juxtaposing two divergent developmental perspectives about transitions from adolescence to adulthood in industrialized societies, the authors invite readers to become a participating audience, and as they make their way through the various chapters of the book and are introduced to the different approaches, theories, and evidence, to join in the playfully serious debate, make up their minds, and become a supporter of one approach or the other: but let no one decide too quickly who are the heroes and who are the villains in the plot!

Changing Societies and the Transition to Adulthood

The lives of young people today have changed almost beyond recognition compared to a half century ago. The age of entering marriage, which formerly was the late teens or very early 20s, is now closer to age 30 in every industrialized country (Douglass, 2005, 2007). The age of entering parenthood has risen more or less parallel to the rise in the marriage age. Premarital sex, formerly strictly prohibited, is now widely tolerated, and in North America and northern Europe, cohabitation before marriage has become normative (Jensen, 2001; Stanley, Rhoades, & Markman, 2006). Young women, formerly restricted to future roles of wives and mothers without a need for education or career, now exceed young men in educational attainment all around the world (Coleman & Schofield, 2007; National Center for Education Statistics, 2009). Postsecondary education and training have become more important than ever before, as the economy has shifted from a manufacturing base to a focus on information, technology, and services.

This book sets out to consider the new features of the transition to adulthood in light of these cultural, technological, and economic changes, which represent crucial, dynamic frameworks within which young people face the challenges and risks of striving to achieve adult status. The range of social processes, such as the development of a "risk society" (Beck, 1992), "detraditionalization" (Heelas, Lash, & Morris, 1996), and "individualization" (Beck, 1992; Furlong & Cartmel, 1997), has had a powerful impact on the meaning and experiences of young peoples' transitions to adulthood. Castells (1998), for instance, observed that the contemporary contours of diffuse social, economic, and cultural conditions present new challenges because people must lead their lives without a "route map." This sociocultural "release" means that young people today are less able to refer to traditional ways of knowledge and experience, and less inclined to rely on the advisory competence of adults.

Modern society now offers young people at least the illusion of flexibility and variety, including the belief that in social life "anything goes!": to marry or not marry, to live in a partnership with a same-sex or opposite-sex partner, to have children as a teenager or late in midlife or not at all, to have a job first and a higher education later or the other way round, or to alternate between both. Almost all choices are reversible—partners, jobs, and dwelling places can be left and replaced.

This destandardized life course has been created by a number of macroso-cial factors, such as fluctuating and uncertain job markets, occupational demands for higher qualifications, and changing social customs and practices. Leisure time has also been affected by the same new technologies and global-ization that have been transforming working life: yesterday computer games, today social-networking websites and Twitter, tomorrow who knows? A greater age span is involved in present-day youth scenes, gender and social class differ-ences are more diffuse, and tastes and styles have fragmented. Young peoples' tastes seem *not* to fall within neat gender, social class, or geographic boundar-ies (e.g., Roberts & Parsell, 1994).

In this state of volatility, there are few, if any, normative shifts required on the part of young people, though this is not restricted to young people alone. Fauske (1996) noted, some time ago, that a kind of search for perpetual youth became apparent, with adults behaving like young people: undergoing cosmetic surgery, going back to college, falling in love with a new partner, starting a new kind of job, having exciting leisure pursuits, and following "youth" fashions. Thus, the distinction between youth status and adult status started to become obscure several decades ago and has continued to fade (Buchmann, 1989).

The Need for New Theories

Due to the increasing destandardization and impermanence of life course paths, traditional theories of human development have become outdated. Take, for example, Freud's (1856–1939) and Piaget's (1896–1980) seminal theories. They do not even consider development beyond the teenage years, and many modern textbooks still treat "developmental psychology" as being synonymous with "Child Psychology."

Although Erikson (1902–1994) and Havighurst (1900–1991) did extend their theories of human development to encompass the whole of the life span, the stages they described no longer reflect the real-life experiences of people today. For instance, Havighurst regarded the period of adolescence, ending around the age of 20, as the time for establishing one's identity and resolving the developmental tasks of choosing a career and gaining emotional indepen-dence, whereas he considered age 35 as the approximate starting point for midlife transitions. Given that many young people today wait until close to age 30 to marry and have their first child—it really is true that "30 is the new 20," as the popular phrase states—it seems obvious that these theories have become obsolete, and that developmental psychology needs a new and different approach to be able to explain life span development in the modern world, with its ever-changing shifts and cultural variations.

Furthermore, these global forces and societal influences may vary between countries. Larson (2002) has indicated that there are many new "adolescences" forming around the world, refracted through distinct circumstances and cultural systems, and not a *single* global youth culture. In the early 1990s, for instance, Kloep and Hendry (1997) described Albanian society in transition, where young people admired Western lifestyles but did not have the means to realize them.

For social scientists interested in the lives of young people, clearly the old theories premised on an entry into stable gender-specific adult roles at about age 20 are no longer adequate for the America and Europe and industrialized Asia of the 21st century. There is a need to rethink and re-conceptualise developmental theories so that the profound changes of recent decades are taken into account. But what should be the nature of this re-conceptualisation? This question is at the heart of this book.

Two Theoretical Approaches

Arnett (2000, 2004, 2006a, 2007a, 2010) and Tanner (2006) have proposed that the changes in the lives of young people can best be understood as entailing the rise of a new life stage, which Arnett termed *emerging adulthood*. A half century ago, young people made the transition from adolescence to young adulthood in relatively short order at around age 20, when most entered the roles most commonly associated with adulthood, mainly marriage, parenthood, and (for young men) stable full-time work. Now, however, the decade from the late teens to the late 20s has changed entirely. It is not a time of entering marriage and parenthood, but a time for having romantic and sexual relationships with a variety of partners, with some of those relationships including cohabitation. It is not a time for entering stable full-time work, but a time of continued education and training to meet the demands of the modern information/technology/services economy, followed by a series of short-term jobs in the pursuit of a job that will be optimally satisfying and fulfilling. The focus is not on making commitments to others but on attaining self-sufficiency (Arnett, 1998). Only after self-sufficiency has been attained, and an extended period of self-focused freedom has been experienced, do emerging adults feel ready to become young adults and take on the full weight of adult responsibilities (Douglass, 2005; Tanner, 2006).

To accommodate variations in development, Arnett (2006b, 2010) proposed that there is not one emerging adulthood but many emerging adulthoods.

That is, emerging adults around the world share demographic similarities, in that they wait until at least their late 20s to enter stable adult roles, and they may share developmental similarities such as focusing on identity explorations. However, their experiences are likely to vary by cultural context, educational attainment, and social class. An important issue for the nascent and burgeoning field of emerging adulthood studies is to explore and describe this variation (Arnett, 2006b, 2007a).

One of the goals of the book is to debate the value of this term "emerging adulthood." Clearly many scholars have found it valuable, as in less than a decade it has become used in hundreds of studies by scholars all over the world (Seiffge-Krenke & Gelhaar, 2008), in fields as diverse as psychology, psychiatry, anthropology, education, medicine, social work, theology, and law (Arnett, 2007a).

Hendry and Kloep (2007a, 2007b) take a different view and argue that stage theories have never been able to embrace (or explain) individual transitions across the life course, because there have always been groups, and subgroups, that deviated considerably from the norms created by traditional developmental psychologists. Hence, as there are no universal stages, stage theories cannot be universal theories. If they are not universal theories, then, at best, they are only partial theories, valid for small groups of people at certain historical times within certain societies. It would also imply that we would need a different stage theory for every culture and a new one for every historical period (thus many theories would go out of fashion very quickly in times of rapid social change). Alternatively, psychology could declare itself as a science solely of Western, white, middle-class people, and treat all "outsiders" as deviations from that norm (pretty much as it once did with regard to women); or it could claim that there are different theories for different people dependent on gender, education, social class, and culture.

Furthermore, according to Hendry and Kloep, using age and age stages to explain human behavior is not very explanatory. The fact that many young people delay the age of first marriage is not *explained* by the fact that they are emerging adults. Hence, inventing a new stage and putting a fancy name to it do not add more to our comprehension of human development than categorizing a group of people on the basis of their age and *describing* some commonalities in their behaviour. For this reason, Hendry and Kloep argue that psychological understanding would be more enhanced if we abolished stage theories altogether and tried to find explanations of the processes and mechanisms that govern human change at any age. They argue that it would be more productive to substitute generalizing descriptions for generalizable explanations, and will suggest some ways of doing this within their chapters in this book.

The Outline of the Book

With this book we have created the opportunity to debate our differences, with Arnett and Tanner on one side and Hendry and Kloep on the other. We will critically comment on each other's views, disagree and put forward alternative ideas, and perhaps even come to some common conclusions. In the course of this debate we will each be utilizing research from the United States, Europe, and further afield to support our arguments, so that the reader can be participant, adjudicator, and supporter of one team or the other, in this friendly, if cutting, academic debate about an until recently neglected period of the life span. A number of illustrative case studies are to be found in Chapters 3 and 5 to provide real life examples of the principles discussed.

The book sets out to describe and analyze the period of "emerging adulthood" (both sides have agreed to use "emerging adulthood" in the book to refer generally to persons aged 18–29) not only in Western societies but also in other cultures. The coverage of supporting evidence for the claims and counterclaims in this book may be somewhat partial due to a dearth of existing research findings about this part of the life course. Nevertheless, we will attempt to provide as comprehensive a picture as possible to argue our separate and collective viewpoints. In the course of the text we will describe the transition to adulthood, offer explanations of findings, critically comment on theoretical frameworks and empirical studies, and, finally, attempt to come to some theoretical agreement—or at least allow our play a dénouement before the final curtain.

Although all four authors knew what had been written in the first five chapters, the rejoinder chapters (6 and 7) and the individual sections of the conclusions (Chapter 8) were not been seen by the rival camp before they were completed. In this way we hope to ensure a genuine debate throughout the book. More specifically, the book is arranged in sections as follows.

Arguments for a Stage

Chapter 2. *Presenting "Emerging Adulthood": What Makes It Developmentally Distinctive?*
    J. L. Tanner and J. J. Arnett

Chapter 3. *Themes and Variations in Emerging Adulthood across Social Classes*
    J. J. Arnett and J. L. Tanner

Arguments for a Process

Chapter 4. *A Systemic Approach to the Transitions to Adulthood*
  M. Kloep and L. B. Hendry

Chapter 5: *Lifestyles in Emerging Adulthood: Who Needs Stages Anyway?*
  L. B. Hendry and M. Kloep

Rejoinders

Chapter 6. *Rejoinder to Chapters 2 and 3: Critical Comments on Arnett's and Tanner's Approach*
  M. Kloep and L. B. Hendry

Chapter 7. *In Defense of Emerging Adulthood as a Life Stage: Rejoinder to Kloep's and Hendry's Chapters 4 and 5*
  J. J. Arnett and J. L. Tanner

Conclusion

Chapter 8. *Bringing Down the Curtain*
  J. J. Arnett, M. Kloep, L. B. Hendry, and J. L. Tanner

We invite the reader to join us and view our presentation of ideas, theories, evidence, and counterevidence, at all times participating in, and assessing, the different performances with reasonable objectivity even if remaining partisan, and being critical, yet retaining a sense of humor and ultimately deciding whether the stage deserves to be highlighted or the process emphasized.

SECTION I

Arguments for a Stage

2

Presenting "Emerging Adulthood": What Makes It Developmentally Distinctive?

Jennifer L. Tanner and Jeffrey Jensen Arnett

The theory of emerging adulthood identifies a new and distinct period of the life course that has come to characterize the experiences of 18- to 29-year-olds in industrialized societies over the past half-century (Arnett, 2000). The shared experiences of young people in their 20s took on new meaning for cohorts that came of age in the 1980s and 1990s and afterward. In prior decades, the 20s were relatively predictable: young people finished their education, moved out of their parents' household, got married, and had their first children all in a short period of time, usually by about age 25. The neat and expected sequencing of the age period, however, has faded.

Prior to Arnett's work identifying the life stage *emerging adulthood* and distinguishing it from both adolescence and young adulthood, a variety of human development theories variously accounted for these years. Erikson's lifespan theory (1950) posited adjoining stages, adolescence (stage 5) and young adulthood (stage 6), during which young people encountered related tasks: *identity vs. identity confusion* and *intimacy vs. isolation*, respectively. In this framework, people between approximately ages 19 and 34 are universally oriented to the resolution of self in relation to others (intimacy) and society (via work). Separate models accounted for development that occurred in college students during these years (e.g., Keniston, 1965, 1971; Perry, 1970). In the 1970s, Sheehey's (1976) and Levinson's (1978) popular works highlighted the transitional nature of the young adult years, noting that for some, the 20s involved a tension for young people that was resolved by making commitments to adult roles.

Macrolevel forces reshaped opportunity structure and value systems in the 1980s resulting in a changed landscape of adulthood. In 1950, relatively few people in any country obtained any higher education, and of those who did nearly all of them were young men. Most young women, as well as many young men, remained in their parents' household until they married in their late teens or very early 20s. The entry to parenthood came about a year later, on average. Thus, most young people went directly from adolescence to a settled young adulthood by their early 20s.

Dramatic shifts in the timing of entering adult roles have occurred since the 1950s. Participation in higher education has risen steeply, especially among young women. Now over half of young people enter postsecondary education or training the year after graduating from secondary school in most industrialized countries, and in nearly every country women obtain more education than men (Douglass, 2007). The median age of first marriage has risen steeply as well, to nearly age 30 across industrialized countries, with a corresponding rise in the median age of entering parenthood (Fig. 2.1, Mathews & Hamilton, 2009). Furthermore, since the Sexual Revolution of the 1960s changes in attitudes toward premarital sex have taken place, and the majority of young persons have sexual intercourse for the first time in their late teens, a decade or more before they enter marriage. In the United States, Canada, Australia, and Northern Europe, over half of young people cohabit before marriage.

Given the changing landscape of the way that young people were spending their years after adolescence and before they committed to marriages and

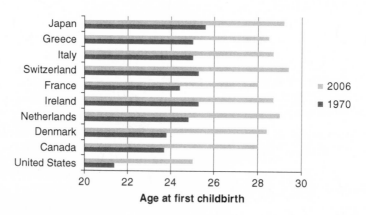

FIGURE 2-1 Trends in the Timing of First Childbirth.

careers, Arnett (2000) advanced a reconceptualization of the transition to adulthood. He argued that a new way of becoming adult became normative at the end of the twentieth century. Moreover, the features of these years required it to be understood as a new stage of development, *emerging adulthood*.

Arnett emphasized from the first articulation of the theory that the rise of emerging adulthood is principally a demographic phenomenon based on later entry into stable adult roles; emerging adulthood is the new life stage that opened up when transitions in love and work that previously took place in the late teens or early 20s moved into the late 20s or early 30s (Arnett, 2000). The theory of emerging adulthood proposed that this stage was distinct not just demographically but subjectively and psychologically from the adolescence that preceded it and the young adulthood that followed. No longer adolescents and not yet adults; *what then?* Arnett emphasized that the content of these years would vary among cultures, but based on his research he proposed that in the United States these years mark the era of (1) seeking identity, (2) experiencing instability, (3) focusing on self-development, (4) feeling in-between adolescence and adulthood, and (5) optimistically believing in many possible life pathways (Arnett, 2004). Research comparing age groups has found these themes to be more prominent in emerging adulthood than in adolescence or later adulthood (Reifman, Arnett, & Colwell, 2006).

What Is Developmentally Distinctive about Emerging Adulthood?

For emerging adulthood as for other life stages, for them to be conceptually useful there should be features that make them distinct. In addition to the five features proposed by Arnett (2004), what else makes emerging adulthood developmentally distinctive? In the remainder of the chapter we address this question. We wish to emphasize that "distinctive" does not mean "homogeneous." That is, to state that a certain characteristic is distinctive to emerging adulthood does not mean that all emerging adults possess it; rather, it means simply that the characteristic is more likely to be found in emerging adulthood than in other stages of life. All life stages are heterogeneous, and emerging adulthood more than any other because of the lack of institutional structure, so we would certainly not propose any characteristics as true of all emerging adults. "Distinctive" also does not mean "universal." We emphasize that emerging adulthood exists as a normative life stage in some cultures but not in others. Furthermore, features that are part of emerging adulthood in one culture may not apply to other cultures. Finally, "distinctive" does not mean "discrete." Most of the qualities we describe in this chapter begin before emerging adulthood and continue afterward, so they are not discrete; they are distinctive because they are more prominent in emerging adulthood than in other stages. With these caveats in mind, we now examine some distinctive features of emerging adulthood, mostly in the North American context, with respect to personality organization, cognitive and neurological development, mental health, and physical health. Then we examine the distinctiveness of emerging adulthood with respect to social relationships to family, friends, and love partners, and in regard to educational paths and the school-to-work transition.

Personality Organization

With regard to personality, increased instability during emerging adulthood and increased stability thereafter distinguish certain aspects of personality development during these years. Although personality traits demonstrate moderate rank-order stability from age 18 to 26 (Roberts, Caspi, & Moffitt, 2001; Robins, Fraley, Roberts, & Trzesniewski, 2001), these years are marked by lower rank-order stability than in adolescence or later adulthood (Roberts, Walton, & Viechtbauer, 2006). Roberts et al. (2006) found that social dominance, conscientiousness, and emotional stability increased more and social vitality decreased more during this age period compared to changes during later adulthood.

Although the extent of personality change is higher in emerging adulthood than before or after, the changes are generally in the direction of greater stability, maturity, and self-control. In terms of ego development (e.g., Loevinger, 1976), maturation of ego including the increasing control of impulses and increasing complexity of understanding the world increases with age through emerging adulthood. Roberts, Caspi, and Moffit (2001) found that from age 18 to 26, emerging adults demonstrate increases in self-constraint, moving away from impulsive behavior to greater self-control, demonstrating more reflective, deliberate, and planful behavior. Reviewing studies of personality change across the life course, Caspi (1998) concluded that "from late adolescence through early adulthood, most people become less emotionally labile, more responsible, and more cautious" (p. 347).

Similarly, agency, sense-of-control, and mastery over one's environment increase across emerging adulthood (Lewis, Ross, & Mirowsky, 1999). As individuals pass through their 20s, they increase in their belief that they can plan and implement strategies to guide their own lives (Schwartz, Côté, & Arnett, 2005). In addition to the overall increase in agency, emerging adults experience an increase in their sense of achievement and social potency, reflecting gains in pleasure derived from meeting environmental challenges (e.g., success in the school-to-work transition).

Cognitive and Neurological Development

One of the most revolutionary areas of discovery in the past two decades has been in the area of brain research. Findings specifically related to emerging adulthood are among the most paradigm-shifting. Coincident with advancements in developmental science, exciting progress in neuroscience has identified significant differences between the adolescent and emerging adult brains (Sowell, Thompson, & Toga, 2004). Cognitive science has, in parallel, progressed in its understanding of emerging adulthood as a critical period for the evolution of adult cognitive structures (Labouvie-Vief, 2006). Evidence of brain reorganization associated with rational decision making substantiates the assertion that emerging adulthood is a unique and critical developmental period.

Recent advances in neuroscience have revealed significant, unanticipated differences between the adolescent and emerging adult brain (Gogtay et al., 2004). It is now understood that the brain's center for reasoning and problem solving reaches maturity during emerging adulthood, accomplished by a pruning of gray matter following adolescence into the 20s (Giedd et al., 1999). Next, there is an increase in white matter across this same period through the mid-30s. This combination results in change toward fewer but faster connections (Gogtay et al., 2004). Thus, adolescence is the final era of brain plasticity, whereas emerging adulthood corresponds to the final phase of organization of the adult brain. Emerging adults experience this as a process of increasing emotion-regulation and ease in decision making as emotion is parsed apart from cognitive processing.

Developmental theorists, prior to our new understanding of brain maturation, identified postadolescent differences in cognitive organizing and processing (Perry 1970, 1981; Schaie, 1977; Labouvie-Vief, 1980, 1985). For example, Perry (1970, 1981) recognized that typical students entering college are likely to think "dualistically" (i.e., seeing issues as black and white) whereas those leaving college are more likely to demonstrate "multiplicity" in their thinking (i.e., understanding that there may be multiple legitimate views of an issue). Schaie's (1977) model of cognitive development differentiates the adolescent *acquisition* stage from the *achieving* stage that dominates in emerging adulthood. The former stage involves collecting information, while emerging adulthood marks the advent of applying and refining knowledge acquired via application of knowledge to real-world situations.

Labouvie-Vief's and colleagues' work and findings are consonant with the theory of emerging adulthood in that the first years of emerging adulthood lack subjective stability, but cognitive and reflective organization increases as individuals transition to adulthood (Labouvie-Vief, 2006). Emerging adulthood is an important age period for the onset and rapid expansion of complex thought structures (Labouvie-Vief, Chiodo, Goguen, Diehl, & Orwoll, 1995; Labouvie-Vief & Meddler, 2002). In contrast to self-descriptions of younger people, emerging adults access higher levels of cognitive understanding of self, such as *dynamic-intersubjective* reflections at which "roles and traits are described at a complex psychological level and reflect awareness of underlying, often unconscious motivation and reciprocal interaction" (Labouvie-Vief, 2006, p. 70).

Lifespan conceptualizations of intellectual development and ways of knowing point to the importance of the emerging adult years for acquiring competence. Attaining wisdom-related knowledge and judgment—expertise in the conduct and meaning of life—occurs primarily during emerging adulthood, from ages 15 to 25 (Baltes & Staudinger, 2000). Declines take place after emerging adulthood across multiple indices of cognitive ability, including numerical ability, verbal aptitude, clerical perception, finger dexterity, and general intelligence (Avolio & Waldman, 1994). Mid-emerging adulthood, there is a point of inflection for cognitive performance at which crystallized intelligence stabilizes (i.e., intelligence as cultural knowledge), but fluid intelligence reaches its peak and then begins to decline (i.e., intelligence as basic information processing; Baltes, Staudinger, & Lindenberger, 1999). During emerging adulthood, knowledge that is culturally relevant and steeped in experience becomes more salient (i.e., pragmatics).

Complementary to crystallized intelligence as measured by IQ tests, other types of intelligence, such as practical and emotional, are specifically associated with emerging adulthood. Practical intelligence is "intelligence as it applies in everyday life in adaptation to, shaping of, and selection of environments" (Sternberg & Grigorenko, 2002, p. 215). Despite less life experience, emerging adults provide better solutions than older adults do to some problems (Hershey & Farrell, 1999), suggesting that inexperience in the adult world does not eliminate the potential that practical intelligence serves as a resource during emerging adulthood.

A Rise in Psychopathology Risk—and in Well-Being

In terms of mental health, a distinctive feature of emerging adulthood is the high rate of psychopathology found in this age group. Emerging adults experience more psychiatric disorder in one year than any other adult age group

(Kessler, Chiu, et al., 2005). A majority (75%) of emerging adults who experience a psychiatric disorder have had a prior episode, at least one, in childhood or adolescence (Kessler, Berglund, Demler, Jin, & Walters, 2005; Kim-Cohen et al., 2003). As well, new cases appear across emerging adulthood (Tanner et al., 2007). Anxiety disorders are most prevalent (22.3%), followed by substance use disorder (22.0%), mood disorders (12.9%), and impulse control disorders (11.9%) (Kessler, Chiu, et al., 2005).

Childhood and adolescent psychopathology exerts significant influence on the course of mental health problems through emerging adulthood (Fergusson & Woodward, 2002; Paradis, Reinherz, Giaconia, & Fitzmaurice, 2006; Tanner et al., 2007). In one longitudinal study, approximately one in five adolescents (22.3%) who met criteria for "high" mental health problems remained in the "high" group 10 years later in emerging adulthood (Hofstra, van der Ende, & Verhulst, 2001). Continuity was even stronger for those who had few problems. Nearly 70% of those "low" in mental health problems in adolescence were classified as "low" in emerging adulthood.

How can this portrayal of emerging adults as being at high risk for psychopathology be reconciled with the view of emerging adulthood as the optimistic "age of possibilities" (Arnett, 2004)? There is a paradox in mental health during this life stage: even as emerging adulthood is a risk period for psychopathology for a minority, it is also a period of rising well-being for most (Schulenberg & Zarrett, 2006). Findings from several longitudinal studies demonstrate increasing well-being and decreasing psychological symptoms across emerging adulthood. Drawing on data from the national Monitoring the Future study, Schulenberg and colleagues (Schulenberg et al., 2000; Schulenberg & Zarrett, 2006) reported increases in perceived social support, satisfaction with life, self-efficacy, and self-esteem, and significant decreases in loneliness, fatalism, and self-derogation from age 18 to 22. Similarly, Galambos and colleagues (2006) found evidence of increases in self-esteem and decreases in anger and depressive symptoms from age 18 to 25 in a Canadian community sample. Moreover, emerging adulthood has been proposed as a "critical period" for the expression of resilience, when many people who had experienced difficult environments in childhood and adolescence rise sharply in mental health once they leave their families (Arnett, 2004; Masten, Burt, Roisman, Obradovic, Long, & Tellegen, 2004; Masten, Obradovic, & Burt, 2006).

Although mental health and well-being rise from adolescence to emerging adulthood for most people, rates of depressive symptoms are higher among people in their 20s compared to all older age groups, except those in their 80s (Mirowsky & Ross, 1999; Vaillant, 2002). In addition, negative affect is highest in the 20s compared to the later adult years (Charles, Reynolds, &

Gatz, 2001). But negative affect begins to decrease in the 20s after reaching its peak, as do feelings of alienation and aggression (Roberts, Caspi, & Moffitt, 2001). In short, the complexity of mental health in emerging adulthood is an important and rich area for future research.

A Respite from Physical Disease

In contrast to mental health problems, rates of serious physical disorders are exceptionally low during emerging adulthood. In 2003, the most recent year for which data are available, only 4% of 18- to 24 year-old Americans self-reported fair or poor health compared to 6% of 24–44 year olds, 12% of 45–54 year olds, and 19% of 55–64 year olds (National Center for Health Statistics, 2005). Predictors of serious physical illness, however, such as obesity and tobacco use, are frequently observed among emerging adults. Negative health behaviors practiced during this part of the life span may provide the foundation for health problems in later adulthood (Merluzzi & Nairn, 1999).

In the past decade, as rates of overweight and obesity in Americans have risen, obesity has become one of the most significant health problems for emerging adults, as well as a predictor of health problems in later adulthood. Although emerging adults have lower rates of overweight and obesity than older adults, being mildly or moderately overweight at ages 20–22 is a significant predictor of obesity by ages 35–37 (McTigue, Garrett, & Popkin, 2002) and being seriously overweight or obese elevates the later risk of heart disease, diabetes, high cholesterol, hypertension, and some types of cancer (National Center for Health Statistics, 2005).

The high rates of overweight and obesity seen among emerging adults may be due, in part, to a lack of physical activity. Research has demonstrated a significant decrease in physical activity during the transition from adolescence to emerging adulthood (Gordon-Larsen, Nelson, & Popkin, 2004), which in turn is associated with obesity later, in young adulthood (Tammelin, Laitinen, & Näyhä, 2004). Furthermore, findings from a population-based, longitudinal cohort study show an inverse relationship between fitness in emerging adulthood and risk factors for cardiovascular disease such as hypertension and diabetes in middle age, even after controlling for body mass index (Carnethon et al., 2003).

Tobacco use is another negative health behavior with serious consequences that is common among emerging adults. Although cigarette smoking is on the decline, approximately one-fourth of American emerging adults still use tobacco. In 2003, approximately 25% of all males and 22% of all females ages 18–24 reported currently smoking cigarettes, contributing to increased risk of later heart disease, stroke, diverse types of cancer, and chronic lung diseases such as emphysema (National Center for Health Statistics, 2005).

Low rates of physical disease during emerging adulthood underlie the 98% survival likelihood between ages 15 and 34 (Anderson, Kochanek, & Murphy, 1997). However, statistics highlighting health and low rates of mortality and morbidity obscure unique causes of mortality during emerging adulthood. Seventy percent of deaths in the 18–25 age group are due to motor vehicle accidents, homicide, HIV infection, and suicide; these causes comprise only 8% of deaths in the overall population (U.S. Department of Health and Human Services, 2000). The impulsive and risk-taking behaviors and incomplete brain development of emerging adults have both been implicated as risk factors associated with the high rate of preventable death in this age group. However, there are notable cross-national differences. In an analysis of countries representing Asia, Europe, North America, Latin America, and Oceania, U.S. mortality rates for homicide and motor vehicle accidents in emerging adulthood were higher than in all other industrialized nations (Heuveline, 2002).

Love and Work: Distinctive Patterns in Emerging Adulthood

In addition to the areas of functioning described above, emerging adulthood is distinctive in terms of the nature of social relationships and patterns of education and work. In the following sections we discuss the distinctiveness of emerging adulthood with respect to family relations, friendships, love partnerships, educational paths, and the school-to-work transition. First, however, we present Tanner's idea of recentering as a framework for understanding the distinctiveness of love relationships in emerging adulthood.

Recentering: A Developmental Systems Perspective on Emerging Adulthood

Complementing Arnett's characterization of the primary features of emerging adulthood, Tanner (2006) articulated the process of becoming adult from a lifespan developmental systems perspective (Baltes, 1987; Lerner, 2002), focusing on pathways of individual development from adolescence through emerging adulthood and into young adulthood. Tanner's model stresses the relational nature of human development, interactions between individuals, and contexts that produce development. Individual pathways of development across emerging adulthood, as with all stages of human development, involve continuities and discontinuities, plasticity, normative and non-normative experiences, and variability in experiences (i.e., individual differences). Development involves both gains and losses.

Tanner introduced the term "recentering" as a label for the three-stage process that involves the transition from adolescence into emerging adulthood (Stage 1), emerging adulthood proper (Stage 2), and the transition out of emerging adulthood into young adulthood (Stage 3) (see Fig. 2.2). Recentering involves individual's shifting their primary involvements away from contexts that supported dependence (e.g., families, schools) to contexts of adulthood, which nourish adult interdependence (e.g., peer and intimate relationships, careers, community). As individuals recenter, they are faced with the developmental challenge of becoming a guide for themselves into and through adulthood. In Eriksonian terms, adaptation is the gain of self-governance.

Stage 1 begins when the adolescent is embedded in contexts of childhood, primarily the family of origin (Fig. 2.2, Stage 1). As restrictions that define the adolescents as "dependent" are lifted and as the adolescent makes life choices of his or her own, the individual progresses through Stage 1 of the recentering process. The beginning of Stage 1 is objectively marked by the legal emancipation of individuals from the responsibility of their parents. By definition, leaving adolescence and entering emerging adulthood is marked by a weakening of familial and institutional ties. Despite a concentration of this occurrence at age 18, a small minority of individuals is emancipated legally as adolescents (e.g., financial emancipation from parents, early graduation from high school), some dissociate from institutional care before age 18 (e.g., runaway youth, those who leave high school before graduation), and a subgroup reverses the dependent role before age 18 (e.g., those who become parents or take on head-of-household responsibilities). Likely, there is additional variation around this transition related to the gender of the individual, his or her developmental history of responsible behavior, and parents' values and behavior regarding the independence of their child. Cultural, religious, and social class differences are also sources that influence the individual's transition out of adolescence.

As adolescents age out of traditional contexts of dependence, they enter emerging adulthood proper (Fig. 2.2, Stage 2), marked by temporary role commitments that serve the purpose of exploration of adult identities. During this stage, emerging adults progress in identity development by trying out different (albeit temporary) commitments, eliminating those that do not fit with their plans and goals. Whereas adolescence is marked by subjective, internalized identity exploration, it is not until emerging adulthood that the active phase of identity exploration begins during which individuals attempt to match their adult sense of self with socially-sanctioned adult roles. The extent to which resources remain available to the emerging adult (i.e., via families

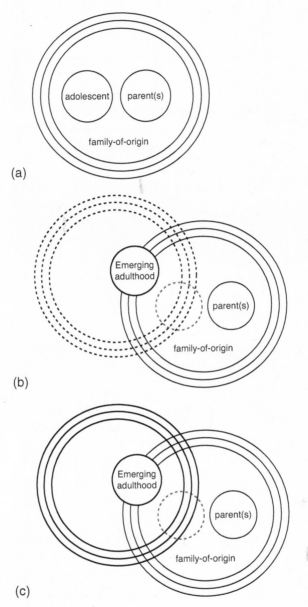

FIGURE 2-2 The recentering process. (a) Stage 1. Launching position: Adolescent transitions from dependent status into emerging adulthood. (b) Stage 2. Emerging Adulthood proper: The emerging adult is peripherally tied to identities & roles of childhood/adolescence; and simultaneously, is committed to temporary identities & roles of adulthood. (c) Stage 3. Young Adulthood: The emerging adult exits stage 2 via permanent identity & role commitments.

and/or institutions) is one source of variation defining how an individual experiences emerging adulthood. Other sources of individual differences in the experience of emerging adulthood are the length of time emerging adulthood is experienced and the level of stress. In addition to resources, opportunities available to emerging adults greatly impact the time spent, the experiences accrued, and the strengths gained during the emerging adult years.

The end of emerging adulthood is marked by Stage 3 of the recentering process (Fig. 2.2, Stage 3), occurring when individuals make enduring commitments to relationships and careers, taking on adult roles and responsibilities. Identity exploration recedes at Stage 3, marking the beginning of identity consolidation occurring around commitments to careers, partners, children, community, and aging parents. Such commitments promote stability of responsibility to these roles, to self, and to others (Whiting, 1998). After the experimentation of emerging adulthood, and the culling of identity options and roles, the task at hand in young adulthood is the reorganization of self around the roles and responsibilities to which an individual has committed.

The process of recentering is useful for understanding not only normative and nonnormative experiences during the first years of adulthood, but presents a framework for predicting more and less successful adaptation during the transition to adulthood. The events and transitions that occur during this age period are likely to be considered, by both younger and older adults, the most significant, key marker events that shape their lives (Elnick, Margrett, Fitzgerald, & Labouvie-Vief, 1999; Grob, Krings, & Bangerter, 2001). Despite the fact that adult event transitions (e.g., marriage, transition to parenthood) are rarely considered significant indicators of being an "adult" (Arnett, 1998, 2001, 2003), these events play an important role in the experience of one's life. Successful adaptation is predicted by the extent to which an emerging adult has choices in the process of selecting adult roles and commitments (Rönkä, Oravala, & Pulkkinen, 2003), as well as the extent to which these commitments "fit" an individual (Lerner, 1984).

Recentering marks a pivotal point in the human lifespan. Prior to emerging adulthood the individual is to a great extent regulated by others. The shift to self-regulation or what Heinz (2009) calls "self-socialization" occurs during emerging adulthood. Emerging adulthood is the critical developmental stage during which individuals select life goals based on available resources and opportunities (Freund & Baltes, 2002; Freund, Li, & Baltes, 1999). Life goals are narrowed, eliminated, and refined (Nurmi, 1993, 1997). Articulating and selecting goals, directing one's resources to achieve those goals, and evaluating one's success in meeting identified goals contribute to emerging adult mental health (Nurmi, 1997). Nurmi and Salmelo-Aro (2002) found that depressive symptoms were reduced when emerging adults who had career goals were able to find jobs; among those who had identity goals, depressive symptoms were reduced when they were engaged in contexts that supported identity exploration. In turn, such person–environment fit is associated with mental health and personality stability (Roberts, O'Donnell, & Robins, 2004).

In sum, recentering describes a normative experience in individual development unique to this age period. Understanding the unique features of this age period identifies the emerging adulthood life stage not only as distinct from other stages of human development, but also as a potentially critical or sensitive period of development.

Renegotiating Family Relationships

As the recentering concept describes, from adolescence to emerging adulthood the parent–child relationship evolves from a pattern of child dependence on parents to a relationship between two adults characterized by equality (Aquilino, 2006). This change in the parent–child relationship is recognized by emerging adults as one of the most important markers in becoming an adult (Arnett, 1998). Renegotiating one's relationship to one's family is the first step of recentering. To some extent, when and how the restructuring of the parent–child relationship occurs are influenced by the residential and financial independence of the emerging adult. Emerging adults leaving home to live independently signals parents that their child is becoming an adult and often leads to reduced conflict and power issues in the relationship (Aquilino, 1997, 2006).

Terms such as "separation" and "individuation" fail to capture the need for and benefit of continued support from families across emerging adulthood. Scabini and colleagues (2006) assert that in European countries, the focus of parent–child relations in emerging adulthood is not on separating from parents but on restructuring the relationship so that emerging adults gain more autonomy even as parents continue to provide both material and emotional support, while mutual closeness and fondness are maintained. In Italy, the specific focus of Scabini et al.'s (2006) research, most Italians continue to live with their parents through their 20s, but—contrary to stereotypes—while doing so they also develop considerable social, sexual, and occupational autonomy. Similarly, in the United States parental support during emerging adulthood is compatible with growing autonomy and with mutual affection and closeness (Swartz & O'Brien, 2009).

Family relationships, particularly between parents and the emerging adult child, and support received from family members have important implications for successful outcomes in adulthood. The developmental tasks of the emerging adult period present a challenge to some, making family support during this transition crucial. Research drawing on a college sample found that both maternal and paternal support predict emerging adult psychological adjustment (Holahan, Valentiner, & Moos, 1994) and support from siblings has been shown to play a role in psychological adjustment as well. High levels of sibling social support are associated with lower levels of loneliness and depression and higher levels of self-esteem and life satisfaction (Milevsky, 2005).

Emerging adults also receive financial support from their parents. In the United States, 2/3 of emerging adults in their early 20s and 40% in their late 20s receive some level of financial support (Shoeni & Ross, 2005). In Europe as well as in the United States, the higher the parents' income, the more money they provide to their children during emerging adulthood (Swartz & O'Brien, 2009).

Friendships

Similar to family relationships, friendship also takes on new meaning in emerging adulthood. In particular, friendships are considered a resource that helps individuals as they pursue mastery of stage-specific developmental tasks (Crosnoe, 2000). For example, competence in friendships in emerging adulthood has been shown to be predictive of competence in young adulthood, not only in friendships but also in the areas of work and romantic relationships (Roisman, Masten, Coatsworth, & Tellegen, 2004). In addition, friendships have significant consequences for emerging adult psychological adjustment and well-being (Bagwell et al., 2005).

Friendships sometimes exceed family relationships in importance during emerging adulthood. In one of the earliest studies of close relationships across the lifespan, Shulman (1975) found that when asked to describe the people who composed their personal network, emerging adults (ages 18–30) were significantly more likely not to name any family members (41%) than were young adults (ages 31–44; 34%) and older adults (over age 45; 23%). In addition, emerging adults report that their relationships with their friends are closer, more important, more reciprocal, and characterized by greater positive feelings than their relationships with their siblings (Pulakos, 2001).

Number of friends remains fairly constant during emerging adulthood, and although the amount of time spent with friends is greatest during adolescence, it stays relatively high during emerging adulthood (Hartup & Stevens, 1999). In addition, studies of emerging adult friendships demonstrate that factors characteristic of adolescent friendships such as loyalty, warmth, and sharing of personal experiences remain important (Samter, 2003).

Friendships in emerging adulthood are strongly influenced by the many transitions that occur during this period of the lifespan. Role changes associated with career entry appear to be related to a partial withdrawal from friends during emerging adulthood (Fischer, Sollie, Sorell, & Green, 1989). Having a romantic partner—or not—is crucial to the place that friends hold in the lives of emerging adults. In one study, single emerging adults reported that friends were their most preferred companions or confidants whereas married persons in the same age group reported that their spouse was the most preferred to fill these roles (Carbery & Buhrmester, 1998). Overall, friendships may reach their peak of functional significance during emerging adulthood. Families are relied on less, and during times when no romantic partner is in the picture friends are most likely to fill the role of companion and confidant and are a primary source of social support (Carbery & Buhrmester, 1998).

Finding "The One": Romantic Partnerships

The transition from adolescence to adulthood is the period of the lifespan when individuals typically form enduring romantic relationships and strive to complete intimacy tasks (Erikson, 1982). The small but growing body of research on intimate relationships in emerging adulthood provides evidence that romantic beliefs and behaviors, rates of partnership, and relationship duration and quality differ from adolescents and older adults (Fincham, 2010). Whereas first kisses, first dates, falling in love, and first sexual intercourse typically occur during adolescence, first serious relationships usually do not occur until emerging adulthood (Regan, Durvasula, Howell, Ureno, & Rea, 2004). Participants in one German longitudinal study were more likely to report having a romantic partner in emerging adulthood (65%) than they were in middle (43%) or late (47%) adolescence, and their emerging adult relationships continued for a longer time (21.3 months) than their relationships in adolescence (5.1 and 11.8 months for middle and late adolescence, respectively; Seiffge-Krenke, 2003).

Romantic beliefs and perceptions also vary by stage of the lifespan. Compared to adolescents, emerging adults are less likely to endorse the romantic belief of idealization (love will be nearly perfect) but do not differ in beliefs of a one and only love partner (there is only one person for each of us) and in love at first sight (Montgomery, 2005). However, emerging adults express higher levels of passionate feelings and intimacy than adolescents (Montgomery, 2005) and perceive their romantic partners as providing more social support

(Seiffge-Krenke, 2003). In a study of romantic love across the life course, Montgomery and Sorell (1994) found that unmarried emerging adults' attitudes toward their relationships were more likely to be characterized by possessiveness and dependency and less likely to be characterized by an altruistic, selfless love than young and middle-aged married adults. In addition, emerging adults reported less relationship satisfaction than older adults. Emerging adults' attitudes did not differ from older adults, however, in terms of physical and emotional attraction or the friendship aspects of love.

A significant proportion of emerging adult romantic relationships involve cohabitation. One study of the timing and decision to enter into a cohabitating union showed that the decision of emerging adults to cohabit is based on finances, convenience, their housing situations, because they simply wanted to, and the anticipated response of parents/family (Sassler, 2004). Surprisingly, living with a partner as a trial or way to determine compatibility for marriage was the least frequently cited reason for deciding to cohabit. However, cohabitation often leads to marriage. The most recent data show that about 60% of current American emerging adults cohabit with at least one partner before marriage, and about half of cohabiting relationships culminate in marriage (Smock & Greenland, 2010). Rates of cohabitation are even higher in Northern Europe, but are very low in Southern Europe (Douglass, 2007).

Education, Careers, and Financial Independence

One of the pathways that is particularly relevant to mapping an individual's development through emerging adulthood is the school-to-work transition. The age at which an individual finishes education and enters the labor market, and the pattern of job-holding that follows the exit from formal education, both account for variation in the school-to-work transition. In 2000, 86.5% of Americans 18 to 24 year olds had completed high school. Of the 13% of emerging adults who had not completed high school by age 24, some persisted in their pursuit of a high school diploma substitute [General Education Development (GED) certificate] into their late 20s (U.S. Department of Education, 2001). In more recent years, rates of leaving high school before earning a diploma have decreased, but race and ethnic differences persist; black and Hispanic youth are more likely to leave high school before earning a degree (Child Trends, 2007).

Rates of high school completion, graduation with associates and bachelor's degrees, as well as advanced professional degrees have each increased significantly during the past century. Currently 30% of 25- to 29-year-old Americans have a 4-year bachelor's degree (National Center for Education Statistics, 2010).

Those who do not enroll in a college program after high school have been labeled the *forgotten half* (William T. Grant Foundation, 1988), because they represent a vulnerable population less likely to make transitions to stable, sustaining employment. Economic prospects of this high-risk group declined from the early 1970s to the late 1990s, as manufacturing jobs declined and the information-technology-service sector of the economy expanded (William T. Grant Foundation, 1998).

Although those who do not complete college may be more vulnerable on some economic measures, some have argued against the "college-for-all" policy, citing the need to focus broadly on connecting high school graduates with specific training and careers that match their interests (Rosenbaum, 2002; Rosenbaum & Person, 2003). One established method for connecting non-college-enrolled youth with training and career opportunities is via adult education and training programs. Overall, 44% of the U.S. population aged 16 and older participated in adult education in 2004–2005; 53% of 16–24 year olds were involved in some form of adult education, higher than any other age group (O'Donnell, 2006). Emerging adults were more likely than older persons to be involved in GED programs and part-time college programs, as well as personal interest courses, and were less likely to be involved in work-related training programs (O'Donnell, 2006).

Disparities in educational attainment in emerging adulthood have implications for wages earned across the lifespan. Lifetime earnings in the United States for individuals with a high school diploma are estimated at $1.2 million, compared to $2.1 million for an individual with a bachelor's degree and $4.4 million for an individual with a professional degree (Day & Newburger, 2002). Earning trajectories indicate that for all degree categories except doctoral degrees, annual earnings for 25–29 year olds are under $50,000. By ages 30–34 the earning trajectories of those with bachelor's degrees and higher accelerate past $50,000/year, continuing to increase through the mid-60s. The earning trajectories of those with associate's degrees and less education never rise above $50,000/year, representing a relatively flat trajectory (Day & Newburger, 2002). Despite the variation by race, ethnicity, and sex in rates of high school and college completion, the earnings differential between high school and college completers is the same across groups (Perna, 2003).

Higher educational attainment has also been linked to establishing career stability. By age 30, 37% of those without a high school degree had not held an employment relationship for 2 or more years at some point since age 18, compared to only 18% of those with a bachelor's degree or higher, despite the former group having a greater number of years of potential employment (calculated from Table 3 of Yates, 2005). The median high school dropout took more than 3 years to start a job that would last a full year, and nearly 11 years before starting a job that would last 3 years. Less than 50% of the high school dropout sample had held a job for at least 5 years at age 35. In comparison, the median high school graduate took 6 years to start a job that would last 3 years and 10 years to start one lasting 5 years. Those with a college degree settled into stable employment much more quickly; within a year and a half after graduating they started a job that would last 3 years and it took them less than 4 years to start a job that would last 5 years (from Table 7, Yates, 2005).

Delay of entry into stable careers has developmental implications for the critical task of gaining financial independence. The challenge of gaining financial stability is not an easy task given that individuals in the emerging adult age group have the lowest earnings, across 19 countries, compared to all other periods of adult labor force involvement (OECD, 1998). Furthermore, career success is associated with adaptation in other areas. Gaining status, gaining power, and achieving financial independence are associated with decreases in negative emotionality and gains in positive emotionality from age 18 to 26 (Roberts, Caspi, & Moffitt, 2003).

Conclusion: Distinctiveness and Diversity in Emerging Adulthood

Across a wide range of areas, emerging adulthood is distinctive as a life stage. From personality development to cognitive development to mental and physical health, and across several types of relationships and roles, emerging adulthood is different than the adolescence that precedes it or the young adulthood that follows it. At the same time, there is a great deal of diversity within emerging adulthood, as the next chapter explores.

3

Themes and Variations in Emerging Adulthood across Social Classes

Jeffrey Jensen Arnett and Jennifer L. Tanner

Although the theory of emerging adulthood has been widely embraced since it was first proposed (Arnett, 2000), like all theories it has had its critics, including Kloep and Hendry. In the view of these critics, a key problem with the theory of emerging adulthood is that it does not apply to all young people in the age period from the late teens through the 20s (Bynner, 2005; Heinz, 2009). Specifically, say these critics, it applies to the middle-class young people who go to university and have enough financial support from parents to experience personal freedom and leisure during these years, but not to the working class and lower class young people who have far fewer options. It is young people in the middle class who are able to experience their late teens and early to mid-20s as self-focused years of identity explorations and who look forward to a future of promising possibilities. In contrast, young people in the lower social classes have no such good fortune, and experience their late teens and 20s as a time of struggling to enter an unpromising and unwelcoming labor market. They look at work not as a form of self-expression and identity fulfillment but as a way to make a living, and hope only to get a stable job that pays a decent wage.

Arnett has emphasized from the beginning the importance of taking education and social class background into account in the study of emerging adults. His research on emerging adults has consistently included people with a variety of educational levels, not just college students (e.g., Arnett, 2001, 2003, 2004). In his first article sketching the theory of emerging adulthood, he argued that one of the benefits of the theory is that it would draw greater research attention to the "forgotten half" of young people who do not attend college or university after secondary school.

> The forgotten half remains forgotten by scholars, in the sense that studies of young people who do not attend college in the years following high school remain rare . . . Emerging adulthood is offered as a new paradigm, a new way of thinking about development from the late teens through the twenties, especially ages 18–25, partly in the hope that a definite conception of this period will lead to an increase in scholarly attention to it. (Arnett, 2000, pp. 476–477)

Elsewhere, Arnett has emphasized that attending college or university marks a crucial turning point in the occupational and social class destiny of emerging adults.

> Beginning in the 1960s high-paying manufacturing jobs became scarcer as technology was developed to require fewer workers and as factories moved overseas for cheaper labor . . . Increasingly, the better-paying jobs have required higher education. But as the economies of urban areas declined, so did the quality of the public schools, leaving children attending those schools ill-prepared for going on to college. Thus in emerging adulthood many of them find themselves . . . in a low-paying, unpromising job, struggling to keep their hopes up. (Arnett, 2004, p. 160)

Consequently, it would not be justified to claim that the theory of emerging adulthood is based on middle-class college students and applies only to them. Nevertheless, there is a serious point of difference here between Arnett and his critics. Both sides acknowledge that educational levels and social class matter in this age period, but how much? Crucially, are the social class differences within the age period from the late teens through the 20s best understood as interesting and important variations within a group that still has enough similarities in common to be called "emerging adults" (Arnett's and Tanner's position)? Or are the experiences of working class young people in this age period so different from the experiences of those in the middle class that they cannot reasonably be said to belong to the same life stage (Kloep's and Hendry's position)?

In this chapter we take a step toward answering these questions. First, we briefly review research showing similarities and differences in this age group with respect to social class. Then, we present four case studies of African Americans in their 20s with various social class backgrounds. In our view, these case studies illustrate that even though there are clear and sometimes dramatic differences in life prospects depending on social class, there is enough similarity across social classes to merit the application of "emerging adulthood" to the age group as a whole.

Emerging Adulthood and Social Class: In Search of Difference

What does the evidence say about the role of social class in emerging adulthood? Overall, there are clear differences between middle-class and working-class emerging adults with respect to demographics, but relatively few differences in the social and psychological variables that have been studied so far. First we look at demographic differences and then at the social and psychological variables.

The Demographic Divide by Social Class

Demographically, the most important difference between middle-class and working-class emerging adults is in their educational attainment. It has long been evident that one of the strongest predictors of whether a young person will attend college or university after secondary school is social class background, specifically the parents' own educational attainment (Breen & Jonsson, 2005). Obtaining or not obtaining further education after secondary school is a crucial dividing point in emerging adulthood, for both the present and the future. In the present it makes for a much different experience of the emerging adult years. Emerging adults who obtain postsecondary education or training usually remain economically dependent on their parents during this time (Aquilino, 2006). In the United States, most of them are employed while they are in college or university (Bozick, 2007), but not enough to be financially self-sufficient.

About half of American emerging adults who enter postsecondary education after high school attend 2-year community colleges and about half enter 4-year residential colleges or universities (Hamilton & Hamilton, 2006). Those who enter residential colleges or universities have a distinctive experience of emerging adulthood. For the first year or two most live in a dormitory with udents, where older adults take care of duties such as preparing the paying the electric and water bills, and cleaning the common living . Consequently, they live in a state of "semiautonomy" (Goldscheider & Goldscheider, 1999), with more autonomy than they had as adolescents but not yet as much autonomy and responsibility as they will have later in adulthood. Their semiautonomy is emblematic of their in-between state as emerging adults, on the way to adulthood but not there yet.

The emerging adult years are considerably different for those who work after secondary school rather than pursuing additional education or combining school and work. Rather than focusing during this time on gaining the credentials that will lead to better-paying job opportunities in the long run, they seek work immediately. Perhaps, in this sense, they get a head start over college attenders in developing job-specific skills and knowledge. However, there is no doubt that their income and occupational prospects are not promising in the long run as a consequence of having no postsecondary credentials. In the past 40 years, as the economy has moved away from manufacturing and more toward information and technology, educational credentials have become more important than ever before to economic success. In the United States, since 1970 the median income for people who have a 4-year college degree has risen slowly but steadily, whereas people who have only a high school degree or less have seen their median wages plunge by over one-third (Halpern, 1998; Hamilton & Hamilton, 2006).

There are also important social class differences with respect to the timing of marriage and parenthood. In the United States, currently the median marriage age is 2 years higher for persons with 16 years or more of education than it is for persons with a high school education or less (Amato et al., 2007). Similarly, the more education emerging adults obtain, the later their timing is likely to be for entering parenthood (Glick et al., 2006). The direction of effects goes both ways here—obtaining more years of education may lead emerging adults to plan for later timing of having their first child, but having a first child may also cause young people to curtail their educational plans, especially if the child in conceived unexpectedly in the late teens or early 20s when most higher education is obtained (Mollenkopf et al., 2005).

Social and Psychological Similarities and Differences across Social Class

Although there are definite differences among emerging adults by social class with respect to demographic variables, there are fewer differences evident with respect to social and psychological variables. However, the available evidence is limited, and many areas remain to be investigated for how social class may or may not be important. Studies by psychologists tend to ignore social class; studies by sociologists emphasize social class but ignore psychological variables. Two areas where evidence is available are views of adulthood and hopes for the future.

Views of Adulthood by Social Class

One frequently studied topic regarding emerging adults has been how they view adulthood, including whether or not they perceive themselves to have reached adulthood. Numerous studies on this topic in a variety of countries have found highly consistent results. During the emerging adult years, specifically ages 18–25, most people respond to the question "Do you feel you have reached adulthood?" with neither "yes" nor "no" but "in some ways yes, in some ways no" (Arnett, 2003; Facio & Micocci, 2003; Macek et al., 2007; Mayseless & Scharf, 2003; Nelson & Barry, 2006). Early studies indicating this pattern led Arnett (2004) to describe emerging adulthood as the *age of feeling in-between.*

As for markers of reaching adulthood, the criteria most widely endorsed are individualistic, specifically *accepting responsibility for yourself, making independent decisions,* and *attaining financial independence.* Also widely regarded as important for adulthood is the readiness for family obligations such as supporting a family financially, caring for a child, and keeping a family physically safe. Interestingly, actually taking on family obligations is not considered important for becoming an adult, but rather the *capability* for taking on these obligations. This pattern of results has been found across American ethnic groups (Arnett, 2003) and in a wide range of countries, including China (Nelson, Badger, & Wu, 2004), Argentina (Facio & Micocci, 2003), the United Kingdom (Horowitz & Bromnick, 2007), Israel (Mayseless & Scharf, 2003), Denmark (Arnett & Hart, 2008), Italy (Arnett & Hart, 2008), Romania (Nelson, 2009), and the Czech Republic (Macek et al., 2007).

Unfortunately, relatively few of these studies have looked at how social class background might be related to the results. In one exception, Arnett (2003) examined the relation between social class and views of adulthood among over 500 Americans ages 21–29 years in four ethnic groups (African Americans, Latinos, Asian Americans, and whites). Across social classes, the most widely endorsed criteria were the same independence-oriented criteria as in other studies: accept responsibility for yourself, make independent decisions, and become financially independent. Some social class differences were found for less-endorsed criteria. Participants from relatively low-socioeconomic status (SES) backgrounds were more likely than participants from relatively high-SES backgrounds to favor criteria related to interdependence (e.g., "Learn always to have good control over your emotions"), norm compliance (e.g., "Avoid becoming drunk"), or family capacities (e.g., "Capable of caring for children").

Social class background was also related to self-perceptions of adult status. Participants from relatively low-SES families were more likely to view themselves as having reached adulthood than participants from relatively high-SES families. This may have been due mainly to taking on more family responsibilities from an early age, especially in single-parent families. Also, persons from lower-SES backgrounds were more likely to become parents relatively early than persons from higher-SES backgrounds, and as noted earlier, becoming a parent at a relatively young age often feels like a sudden and irrevocable thrust into adulthood (Arnett, 1998).

Social Class and Hopes for the Future

A key feature of emerging adulthood as proposed by Arnett (2004) is that it is a time of high hopes and expectations, the *age of possibilities*. According to Arnett (2004), emerging adults are highly optimistic because they are at a time of life when they are thinking about the form their adult lives will take, yet few of the actual decisions and turning points that will determine the structure of their adult lives have been reached. Consequently, it is easy for them to imagine a future in which everything works out just as they envision. In emerging adulthood, dreams are cheap because they have not yet been tested in the fires of reality.

But is this true for all or at least most emerging adults, or only for those who have the advantages of a middle-class background, including access to higher education credentials? In the view of some critics, including Hendry and Kloep (2007a, 2007b), optimism during emerging adulthood depends crucially on social class. Young people who are middle class are optimistic, and with good reason, as they have the advantages that go along with their class status, not only higher education credentials but also the social capital that provides connections to promising jobs that pay well. In contrast, young people in the working class have little reason to feel optimistic, because they are excluded from the wide range of opportunities available to their middle-class counterparts. They have little to look forward to in their 20s or beyond, because their occupational options are limited to low-paying drudge work.

Clearly, these are two very different ways of characterizing views of the future in emerging adulthood. What does the evidence say? Our view is that the available evidence shows that optimism is widespread among emerging adults, across social classes. We would readily agree that the real occupational options available to emerging adults who have no higher education credentials are limited and are growing more limited all the time in an economy that is increasingly based on information and technology rather than manufacturing. However, few emerging adults are pessimistic about their prospects, even if they lack these increasingly important credentials.

One piece of evidence comes from a national survey in the United States showing that 96% of 18–24 year olds agreed with the following statement: "I am very sure that someday I will get to where I want to be in life" (Hornblower, 1997). Now, 96% is an enormous proportion, rarely found on any survey question. It means that *almost all* emerging adults in the United States are optimistic about how their adult lives will turn out. They are not just hopeful, they are "very sure" that they will get what they want in life, that what they hope for will become reality.

It is important to interject here that this does not mean that everything is going well for them in the present. As noted in the previous chapter, well-being generally rises steadily in the course of emerging adulthood for most people, but rates of certain kinds of mental disorders are higher during emerging adulthood than during other periods (Tanner et al., 2007). Even for emerging adults without a diagnosable mental disorder, the emerging adult years can be stressful as they struggle to sort out identity issues and to make do with the meager income they get from their low-level jobs, plus a little money from their parents if they are lucky. But it is striking that even if the present is far from rosy, the future looks bright to nearly all American emerging adults.

There is some evidence that coming from a lower social class background may make emerging adults more rather than less optimistic. Arnett (1997, 2004) asked emerging adults if they believed their adult lives would be better or worse than their parents' lives had been. As shown in Table 3.1, a majority

TABLE 3.1 "Do you think your life overall is likely to be better or worse than your parents' lives have been?"

	Percent		
	Better	Same	Worse
African Americans	79	14	7
Latinos	66	26	9
Asian Americans	65	30	4
Whites	52	36	12

Source: Arnett (2004).

believed their lives would be better than their parents' lives had been, across ethnic groups, and very few believed their lives would be worse. Furthermore, statistical analyses indicated an inverse relation between optimism on this question and social class: the lower the emerging adults' social class background (as measured by mother's educational attainment), the higher their optimism that their lives would be better than their parents' lives had been. Qualitative interviews indicated that the primary reason for the optimism of emerging adults from lower social class backgrounds was that they were confident that they would receive more education than their parents had received, and consequently they would exceed their parents in income and occupational success. Thus, the overall spread of participation in higher education that has taken place in the United States over the past half century is reflected in the optimism of individual emerging adults.

What about the emerging adults who do not obtain higher education? They may be somewhat less optimistic than those who do obtain higher education, but their optimism is nevertheless high. For example, Mollenkopf and colleagues (2005) interviewed an ethnically diverse sample of people ages 18–32 and found that optimism was widespread regardless of social class background. African Americans and Latinos had the lowest educational attainment (as they do nationally), but they did not see this as an obstacle to success. African Americans most often declared the goal of owning their own business, even though their parents had the lowest rate of self-employment of any of the ethnic groups.

Could it be that high optimism in emerging adulthood is mainly an American phenomenon? After all, Americans are well-known for their optimism. The "American dream" is a rosy view of the future, promising economic success and personal well-being in return for hard work and self-discipline. However, it could be that this optimism is shared by young people in other affluent countries and in developing countries with high rates of economic growth. Recent research on Chinese emerging adults found them to be even more optimistic than American emerging adults (Nelson & Chen, 2007). Perhaps emerging adults in many countries are optimistic because they share the developmental status of being on the threshold of entering adulthood but not yet having had their visions of the future collide with less friendly realities.

Arnett's recent data on emerging adults in Denmark show that they are every bit as optimistic as their American counterparts (Arnett & Hart, 2008). Like the Americans, young Danes (ages 17–20 years) almost unanimously (95%) agreed that "I am very sure that some day I will get to where I want to be in life." On other items, too, Danish emerging adults were highly optimistic, including in their beliefs that their lives would be better than their parents' lives had been.

Like the Americans, Danish emerging adults from lower social class back-grounds were *more likely* to state that they believed their lives would be better than their parents' lives had been, compared to those from higher social class backgrounds. Otherwise, there was little relation between social class back-ground and views of the future. Across SES groups, Danish emerging adults generally viewed their present and future lives positively. With regard to their current educational status—representing their likely social class destination—Danish emerging adults attending trade schools were slightly less optimistic than those attending the university-preparatory "gymnasium," but were also less likely to see their current lives as a time of instability and anxiety.

Social Class and Emerging Adulthood: Four Profiles

Overall, then, social class has been found to be significantly related to certain aspects of emerging adulthood, but not in ways that notably challenge the framework of Arnett's theory. There is a wide range of educational attainment among emerging adults, but Arnett (2000, 2004) never portrayed higher education as an essential part of emerging adulthood and his theory is based on research with diverse samples of American emerging adults, many of whom obtained no higher education. Emerging adults who obtain relatively less edu-cation tend to marry and become parents about 2 years earlier than college-educated emerging adults in the United States, but this still leaves a period of at least 6 years between the end of secondary school and the entry into the adult roles of marriage and parenthood, and 6 years are certainly an adequate span for a distinct developmental period. Social class is somewhat related to self-perceptions of adult status, with emerging adults from lower social class backgrounds perceiving themselves as reaching adulthood earlier than emerg-ing adults from relatively higher social class backgrounds; however, the most valued criteria for adulthood are the same across social classes. Optimism, too, is something that is pervasive in emerging adulthood and stretches across the social class spectrum.

Still, the available evidence on the relation between emerging adulthood and social class is limited at this point, and many gaps remain to be filled in. In the remainder of this chapter, we present four profiles of emerging adults, with the goal of generating ideas and insights about what some of the most important similarities and differences might be among emerging adults from higher and lower social classes. The interviews are taken from the study that was the basis of Arnett's (2004) book on emerging adulthood and all were con-ducted by Arnett.

All four of the persons profiled are African Americans. We chose African Americans because in the United States, social class issues are displayed most vividly in this ethnic group. In recent decades there has been a pronounced growth in the size of the African American middle class. Nearly one-third of African American families have incomes above the median for white families (Schaefer, 2006), and so could be considered middle class. Yet the poverty rate among African American families is also high, 20% compared to 11% for whites (Lamb, Land, Meadows, & Traylor, 2005). Consequently, if there are pronounced social class differences in the nature—or existence—of emerging adulthood, they are likely to be evident in the lives of African Americans.

We begin with two profiles of young men and then present two profiles of young women.

Carl: "I'd Like to Be the Best Human Being That I Possibly Could Be"

Carl is 23 years old and lives with his parents in San Francisco. His background is working class. His father has worked for the city electric company for 30 years as a lineman, repairing damaged or defective electrical lines, and his mother is a physician's assistant. Currently, Carl is working as a sales person in a retail computer store, a job he calls "not the most thrilling career." However, he is also working toward a college degree in computer science and expects to obtain it within the next year.

He likes computers and wants to pursue a career in that area, but he is still in the process of forming a more specific work identity. When asked how he saw his life 10 years from now, he first responded: "I haven't the foggiest notion to be honest with you." After we talked about it a bit more, it turned out he did have a vision for his work future. "By then, I will hopefully have started, actually, my own consulting company" in data base programming.

In love, too, his identity was clearly still in progress. When asked about his love life he stated emphatically that he is single, but otherwise he was reticent on the topic. "There's people I go to, you know, from time to time, and that's the best I can do for you."

The instability found in many emerging adults' lives is evident in Carl's life, too. He left home at age 18 to attend the University of Mississippi, but dropped out after 2 years because he decided that San Francisco is "the place to be" for someone like him who is interested in computers. Now he has moved back home and changed universities, and his life will change again when he graduates and seeks a new job with his newly minted college degree.

Although neither of Carl's parents was educated beyond high school, they strongly supported higher education for Carl and his siblings. "My father said you should go to college, and he really, really stressed that." Even though his parents did not have much money to spare, they "actually some way or another found some cash somewhere" to allow him to pursue a college degree.

Carl had the sense that living in an area with so much high-tech economic activity would allow him access to social capital. "I found that as far as career-wise, it would be better for me to be around here because I can meet a whole lot of people here that can get me jobs down the road." He had a similarly prac-tical view of his education. The credential of a college degree would be valuable, even if the knowledge obtained from it was not really necessary. "There are excellent opportunities in the computer industry for people that have a high school education, because it's really based more on results, on what you can do. But I think that in the corporate world the first thing they look at is your degree."

living @ home

Carl is a classic emerging adult in terms of feeling in-between. Asked if he believed that he had reached adulthood, he responded, "Not absolutely, because I still sometimes get up in the morning and say, 'Good Lord! I'm actually a grown up!' 'Cause I still feel like a kid." Like many emerging adults he defined adulthood in terms of "being able to take responsibility for your decisions," and he admitted that "I'm not willing to take responsibility for all the things in my life, even though I know I should."

Still, he is in no particular hurry to reach adulthood. He is making the most of his self-focused freedom, even if he feels a little guilty about it some-times. "I've done things like just got up one morning and said, you know, 'I'm going to Mexico,' and just get up and go. And I should have been doing other things."

Carl sees the future as presenting a wide range of possibilities, and his optimism was evident in his forecast that he would be running his own data base consulting firm in 10 years. His goal for life was to fulfill his potential: "I'd like to be the best human being that I possibly could be."

Carl had no sense of being excluded from opportunities because of his parents' working class status. He had already obtained more education than they did and seemed headed toward a higher social class destination. However, in his view, as a black man he would always be a target of discrimination, no matter what his economic status. As a computer sales person, he was reminded on a daily basis of how white people view him. "I get the impression that most white people think I don't know shit." He recounted a story of a time when he had been running home from a girlfriend's house in the early hours of the morning and was picked up by the police as a suspect in a crime. He did not resist, because "most black folks know that late at night, you don't argue with the cops." Although they let him go after a few hours, the experience left him feeling humiliated and angry. Asked if he believed that Africans Americans have equal opportunity in American society, he said "No. Well, if that was so true, you could come down to my neighborhood and go tell all the guys on the corner they have equal opportunity." For Carl, it was race rather than social class that loomed as an obstacle to future success.

Gary: Crab in a Bucket

Gary's life started promisingly enough, with a father who was in the Navy and a mother who worked as a nurse, along with a brother and sister he loved (and still loves). However, his family life soon went awry; his mother suffered a "nervous breakdown" when he was a baby that has incapacitated her ever since, and his father became an alcoholic and left the family. The family slipped from the middle class into poverty, and Gary grew up in shoddy public housing and rough neighborhoods.

Now, at age 29, his life is unstable bordering on chaotic. He has no regular residence. Instead, he circulates among the households of his mother, brother, and grandmother. Where he ends up on a given night is unpredictable. "I just go ahead and crash out, wake up in the morning . . . I really don't have no real set place, as far as my own place, but I'm trying to work on that."

Although he is 29 years old, Gary shows no signs of entering the stable adult roles in love and work that usually characterize the transition from emerging adulthood to young adulthood in the late 20s. He does not have a girlfriend, and in fact has never had one. "I've never been a relationship-type of person." Still, he seems to have a good idea of what he is looking for. "It all starts out with just trust and love. And basically as I look at it the foundation is a friendship, you know, open lines of communication where you're comfortable and can speak whatever's on your mind. And once you get to that point, everything else falls into place. So that's all I been lookin' for—somebody I can really just share my thoughts and feelings with and then won't feel like I'm getting negative input."

He works as a "repo assistant," copying documents, an unfulfilling job to say the least. "It's just a real tedious job. It's the same thing over and over again." He acknowledges that the job is nothing to celebrate. "It's more of a first time out of high school type of thing. You goin' to school, it's a nice little job to have, but as far as making a career out of it, it's not a good job to have." Still, it serves the important function of giving him something to do and helping him avoid trouble. "It's just somethin' to keep some money in my pocket, have somewhere to go during the day time and not put myself in an environment to actually do bad for myself."

Gary has learned from hard experience what can happen as a consequence of being in "an environment to actually do bad for myself." As a teenage boy, he was part of a group of boys who were involved in a wide variety of crimes, from the relatively innocuous (stealing bags of potato chips from the back of a delivery truck) to the serious (stealing automobiles). "One of my cousins had a chop shop, and then we'd steal cars and bring them to him, and he was givin' us $500 a car." Several times he was caught for one infraction or another, and each time he was put on probation, until finally he was picked up in a drug bust and sent to prison.

Looking back now, Gary sees his prison sentence as a key turning point in his life—for the better. "I was really bad off 'cause I was doin' a lot of drugs, smokin' marijuana, cocaine, cigarettes, puttin' cocaine in the marijuana and smokin' it, put cocaine in tobacco, roll it up in a zigzag, smokin' it, and I drank a lot of alcohol and all that . . . When I finally sat down in jail and looked at my life to that point in time, I thought to myself, I really didn't get arrested, I got rescued."

Once his mind cleared and he was able to consider his life from a distance, he concluded that he had been led wrong by a corrupt environment. "You're not really fucked up, you're just in a bad situation. If you get yourself out of that situation, you can do better. You're just caught up in an environment where they keep on pullin' you down. It's like a crab in a bucket. It's like somebody always grabbin' your last leg and pullin' you back in, and never want to see you get out. So I looked at it from a positive standpoint to try and change myself to be better."

However, getting out of that bucket has proven to be difficult. When he left prison in his early 20s, he had little education, few skills, and the stigma of a prison record. Finding a good job with little education or training is difficult; add a felony conviction and prison time, and the obstacles look insurmountable. "See, the scary thing about it is when you go to apply for a job, you put down that felony, most people would not even consider your application." Every time he applies for a job, he faces a dilemma when he reaches the question "Have you ever been convicted of a felony?" He can lie and respond "no," and be disqualified if they check his record. Or he can respond "yes" and be rejected immediately. Given these unpalatable choices, he chooses neither and leaves the question blank.

Gary admits that his life at age 29 is not what he wanted it to be. "I thought I'd be a lot better off, honesty. I thought I'd be doin' somethin' more productive with myself as far as havin' more money, more stable, more financially secure, a career-oriented job by the time I was 30, lookin' to start havin' kids when I hit 30." Nevertheless, he has not lost hope, and sees at least the possibility of a brighter future ahead. "I'm tryin' to change. And the only thing I can do is just think about the things that I'm doin' on that day and do the things that I need to do . . . I feel if I can just put a little bit more effort into my financial situation and just try to stay out of jail, try to get a good job. By the time I hit 40, I should be a whole person as far as knowin' more."

In its outline, Gary's story is all too familiar: a young black man who grew up in a poor family headed by a single mother, got involved in crime with his friends, served time in jail, and now finds that he is 29 years old with grim prospects. However, in terms of social class, his background is more difficult to classify. His origins are middle class, with a father in the Navy and a mother who worked as a nurse, but the family was downwardly mobile from the time Gary was a baby, and he grew up poor. Nevertheless, his sister and brother made it back into the middle class. Both have college degrees. His sister works in a corporation and is happily married. His brother became involved in crime in adolescence, as Gary did, but was given the alternative of entering the military or going to prison. He chose the military, where he learned computer skills that he has parlayed into a lucrative postmilitary career. Gary's struggles in emerging adulthood, then, are attributable not only to his social class origins but to the lack of happy accidents that favored his sister and brother, the contingencies of an individual life.

Erica: "I Was Spoiled"

You could say Erica grew up in the middle class, but the truth is considerably more complicated. Her mother and father divorced when she was a baby, and she never knew her father. Soon her mother remarried, to a white man, and this is the man she calls her father, although he is technically her stepfather. He is an attorney, and the family lived a comfortable life through Erica's childhood. However, when Erica was in her second year of college her parents went bankrupt. "He didn't invest well," Erica explains, "and she was overspending." Suddenly they could no longer provide money for her education. For the next 3 years she worked and struggled to put herself through college, finally graduating 2 months ago.

Surprisingly, Erica sees this jarring decline in her family's financial fortunes as positive for her. "It was the best thing for me," she says, "because I was spoiled. I took advantage of things." Being abruptly cut off from her parents' finances required her to draw on her own resources of hard work and determination. "I really had to learn a lot more about myself."

Now, at age 23, she is a college graduate, but is struggling anew in the work world. "I hate my job!" she exclaims when asked about work. "It's very repetitious. It's not stimulating at all. There's no opportunity for growth there." She works as a legal assistant in a law firm, a job she got through a temporary employment agency (not through her stepfather the attorney). She answers phones, makes copies, does errands, whatever the attorneys need. Her college degree is in public policy and social welfare, but when she looked into jobs in social service agencies she was dismayed to find that "a lot of them are nonprofit, and they pay less than what I'm making. They don't pay very well at all."

Because she is dissatisfied with her current work and her apparent options, she is thinking of going to graduate school. However, she admits that "I don't even know if I want to go back to school. And I want to make more money." What might she study in graduate school? She mentions art school, the health care field, and the fashion industry. "But, you know, I really need to determine between now and then what I want to do cause I will not succeed if I just go back to do something that I don't like." Clearly her work identity is still unformed.

A more definite goal, 10 years from now, is to be "married with kids. I want tons of children, like five. And I would not mind, like, being a homemaker. I mean, I want my husband to be a professional. And I'm willing to work outside the home, too, or go back to work after my kids are five or six or something. But, I mean, family's really important to me. And if we can afford a lot of kids, then I would have a lot of kids."

One moment, she sounds like she is in no immediate hurry to embark on that plan. "I mean, that's 10 years, though. I'm not saying right now that's for me, you know. Between now and then, I want to experience as much as I can. I mean, I want to experience other things. I want to be well rounded." However, a few moments later she says, "I want a boyfriend. It takes too much energy to be dating all these people. It's tiring. I really want to get married. I mean, I have wedding books at home."

She is confident her life will be better than her parents' lives have been. "I'm gonna marry a man I really, really love," she says, and contrasts herself with her mother, whom she sees as having married mainly for money. She also expects to avoid her parents' financial calamities. "I'm gonna handle my financial things better, 'cause that added way too much stress in their life."

Erica's life has great promise, with a college degree in hand and her personal qualities of optimism and determination. However, her current life is one of classic emerging adult instability, to say the least. In both love and work, she is unsettled and her future is unclear. She has a sense of being partly adult but definitely not all the way there. "I feel like I'm an adult in many ways, like the responsibilities I may take on. But there's so many other ways that I'm so

naive, so childish." Her identity is a work in progress, most recently represented in an impulsive decision to change her hair style. "I cut all my hair
off this weekend, I mean, 'cause I was freaking out. I woke up on Sunday thinking, 'I need a change.' Chop, chop, chop."

Like many emerging adults, Erica is ambivalent about this stage of her life,
embracing the freedom of it even as she finds the instability of it aggravating.
"This stuff drives me crazy. Like now is the worst stage. The best, in terms
of there's a lot of room for me to do whatever, and the responsibility is to myself.
But, on the other hand, it's driving me crazy."

Monique: A Car, a House, a Little Dog

The key event in Monique's life took place at age 7, when her family broke up
and she moved with her mother and brother into the housing projects in
Oakland for low-income families. Previously, her family had lived in a decent
lower middle-class area of suburban Los Angeles, where her father worked
as a butcher. However, as Monique describes it, "My father used to sell weed
and stuff, and it was like the Black Mafia had wanted him to join, and he didn't
want to get into that. And so we had to run." He left the family soon after the
move to Oakland and her parents divorced.

Living in the projects placed Monique in an environment with many snares
and risks, and sent her life on a downward spiral from which she is now trying
to escape, at age 27. With her father's income gone, the family slid into poverty
and lived on social welfare payments throughout the rest of her childhood.
Her mother had health problems, so Monique had most of the responsibility
for caring for her younger brother, making it more difficult for her to attend
to her own education. Her early responsibilities made her reach adulthood
faster than usual. "I think that's what an adult is, how to be responsible. I was
always responsible for my brother, so I grew up real fast."

When she was 15 years old, she became involved with a 29-year-old man.
"I guess I looked up to him as a father figure 'cause my father had left us," she
says now. Before long she was pregnant, and she gave birth to her first child at
age 16. The pregnancy was not unexpected, and in some ways she welcomed it.
"It was fun. I had a lot of help. My mom helped me a lot." Still, Monique recognizes that having a child at a young age impeded her education. She dropped
out of high school when she became pregnant, then "I went to a computer
learning center for awhile, but I was pregnant with my son so I dropped out of
there. And then I tried accounting for a minute, but my child care wasn't right.
I was supposed to go to college, but then I got pregnant again."

Now that her children are 11 and 7 years old, she is determined to make her way into the work force. However, this goal is impeded not only by her lack of education, her lack of work experience, and her responsibilities for two children, but by another legacy of the older boyfriend she had as a teenager: an addiction to crack cocaine. "He started me out and it just went on." She has found the addiction extremely difficult to break, but now—after 11 years—she feels she has finally begun to shake it through participation in a religiously based program. "They got me into prayer, more prayer. And I think that helped a lot." Still, she has no illusions that the temptation is gone and she is in the clear. "It doesn't happen overnight. People just stop for years and fall back. It's something you have to fight all your life."

Her dream for her adult life is a simple one, but given her history, daunting and elusive. Right now her children live with her mother and she lives with her father, so that she can try to get a stable job without the responsibilities of caring for her children on a daily basis. She would like to reunite with her children and her partner (who is also the father of her second child) in a household of their own. "I want to move from the city and get into a quiet, nice little place," far from the perils of American lower-class life. She hopes someday to have "a car, a house, a little dog. Typical dream, I guess."

Is Monique an emerging adult despite having her first child at age 16, or not? There is no easy answer to this question. She shows some of the features we have described as common among emerging adults, such as instability and maintaining high hopes (despite many setbacks). However, having a child is the point of no return for entering adulthood, at least for young people who keep the child and care for it. In Monique's case, her social class background put her on a path to early parenthood, and early parenthood not only shut off her emerging adulthood but curtailed her adolescence, as she quit high school and focused on raising her child. She never had the period in between the end of adolescence and the taking on of adult responsibilities that defines emerging adulthood. However, she is trying to get it back now, in some form, by leaving her children with her mother while she attempts to make her way into the work force.

Conclusion: The Complexities of Social Class

Social class is unquestionably an important element in the lives of emerging adults, as it is in the lives of people of other ages. Specifically, the pursuit of postsecondary education structures the lives of some emerging adults but not others, and this difference has repercussions for their lives in emerging adulthood and beyond. For those who pursue postsecondary education, their lives are structured around going to classes and doing course work. Many of them work at least part-time as well, to support themselves and to pay for educational expenses, which can make for a very busy life. Those who are not in school but are working or seeking a job face the formidable challenge of finding a well-paying, enjoyable job without educational credentials, at a time when such jobs are increasingly elusive. Furthermore, future prospects vary greatly for these two groups, with those pursuing postsecondary education having a higher likely social class destination than those who do not, in terms of income and occupational status.

The case studies here illustrate the substantial influence of social class background in how emerging adulthood is experienced, and also how social class is not as simple a variable as it is often portrayed. Carl and Erika came from backgrounds of relative advantage. Carl's parents received no postsecondary education, yet they stressed education and were able to support him financially as he pursued his college degree. Erika's parents were well-off and she grew up in conditions of material comfort, although their bankruptcy while she was in college pulled the financial rug out from under her and made her struggle to support herself so that she could finish her college education.

Gary and Monique grew up in a lower social class than Carl or Erika, and the effects of this on their lives by their 20s are painfully evident. Gary slid down the path unfortunately common among young African American men in urban areas, becoming involved with friends in crime and drugs, culminating in prison time. Monique fell into the life unfortunately common among young African America women in urban areas, becoming a single mother at a young age and addicted to drugs, making it difficult to build a life of her own in her 20s. She lost her opportunity to experience emerging adulthood fully and will never get it back.

Both Gary and Monique fell into problems that were very clearly the consequence of their bleak social class conditions. Put Gary into Carl's childhood environment, and Monique into Erika's, and it is impossible to believe that by their late 20s he would have ended up a drug addict and convicted felon and she would have ended up a drug addict and single mother. For Gary and Monique, their human potentials have been stunted and twisted by a grim set of social class conditions. Both still strive to rise above their environments—the optimism of emerging adulthood shines through even for them, although barely—but by now it is difficult to be optimistic on their behalf. Drug addiction, felony conviction, single motherhood, and poor education—these are weights that can drag even the most determined crab back into the bucket.

Although social class is crucial to how the years 18–25 are experienced, people in this age range can be designated as emerging adults across social classes. At its core the birth of emerging adulthood over the past half century is a demographic phenomenon, arising from the substantial increase in median ages of marriage and parenthood in every industrialized country. A half century ago most people entered these roles at age 20–22, placing them in "young adulthood" right after adolescence, with adult responsibilities of coordinating family life with a spouse, including running the household, paying the bills, and caring for children. Now that the median ages of entering marriage and parenthood have moved into the late 20s or even the early 30s, a stage of emerging adulthood has opened up between adolescence and young adulthood during which people are more independent of their parents than they were as adolescents but have not yet entered the roles that structure adult life for most people. Young people in lower social classes may enter these roles a year or two earlier than their peers in the middle and upper classes, but for most that still leaves a period of at least 6 years between the end of secondary school and the entrance to adult roles, certainly long enough to be called a distinct life stage.

Arnett's (2004) research has indicated that there are other similarities among American emerging adults across social classes, beyond the demographic similarities. For both the lower/working class and the middle class, the years from the late teens through the 20s are a time of trying out different possibilities in love and work, and gradually making their way toward more stable commitments. For both groups, instability is common during these years as frequent changes are made in love and work. For both groups, their hopes for the future are high, even though the real prospects for those with relatively low education are not as promising. However, other features of the age period may be found to vary between social classes within the same country as well as between cultures and countries. Emerging adulthood is growing as a worldwide phenomenon (Arnett, 2007a, 2007b), in demographic terms, and there is sure to be a great deal of variation worldwide in how it is experienced.

A useful analogy can be made here to the life stage of adolescence. Cross-cultural studies, most notably Schlegel and Barry's (1991) study of 186 cultures, have found that in nearly all human cultures, adolescence exists as a period between the time puberty begins and the time adult roles are taken on. However, the length of adolescence and the nature of adolescents' experiences vary vastly among cultures. Some adolescents attend secondary school and some drop out or never go (Fussell & Greene, 2002; Lloyd, 2005). Most live in the same household as their parents, but some become "street children" and live among other adolescents in urban areas (UNICEF, 2003). Some marry by their mid-teens, especially girls in rural areas of developing countries, whereas others will not marry until after adolescence and a long emerging adulthood. Consequently, it makes sense to speak not of one adolescent experience but of *adolescences* worldwide (Larson, Wilson, & Rickman, 2010). Yet we still recognize adolescence as a life stage that exists in nearly all cultures, in some form.

In the same way, we can state that there are likely to be many emerging adulthoods and many forms the experience of this life stage can take depending on social class, culture, and perhaps other characteristics such as gender and religious group (Arnett, 2011). Some emerging adults obtain postsecondary education and some do not. Some live with their parents and some do not. Some experience a series of love relationships, whereas others live in cultures in which virginity at marriage is prized and love relationships before marriage are discouraged. Yet emerging adulthood can be considered to exist wherever there is a period of at least several years between the end of adolescence— meaning the attainment of physical and sexual maturity and the completion of secondary school—and the entry into stable adult roles in love and work.

At this point, emerging adulthood is not nearly as widespread as adolescence. It exists as a normative life stage in economically developed countries. However, in developing countries it exists only among the small but growing urban middle class, and not in the more populous rural areas, where even adolescence is often brief and adult roles and responsibilities are entered by the mid-teens for many people. Nevertheless, in developing countries around the world the urban middle class is likely to continue to grow in the decades to come (Arnett, 2006b, 2007b). It may be that a century from now emerging adulthood will be a normative life stage worldwide, although it will continue to show variations within and between cultures, as adolescence does today.

Arguments for a Process

4

A Systemic Approach to the Transitions to Adulthood

Marion Kloep and Leo B. Hendry

Introduction: Transitions

In this chapter we present a theoretical perspective, which is distinctly different from the stage theory described by Tanner and Arnett in Chapter 2. Instead of arguing for a new life stage to be inserted into the life course, we will propose abandoning the concept of stages altogether, and, instead, will focus on the processes and mechanisms of developmental change.

It would seem at first sight to be fairly straightforward to consider the transitions from adolescence to adulthood. However, if we take a second look, the notion of transitions is somewhat complicated to understand. For example, what exactly is a "transition"? Dictionaries may describe it as "the process of moving from one place to another," which is an acceptable definition, if we are discussing a car traveling from A to B or someone crossing a border from one country to another. If we speak about human development, however, it becomes more difficult to imagine what "movement" we are discussing, or, for that matter, what starting point we envisage and what the end goal may be.

Perhaps it is easier to grasp the ideas we are trying to convey by considering an example. Imagine a river flowing along. We can see eddies, currents, and calm backwaters, how the river divides as it encounters a rock, how different streamlets emerge round the rock then, perhaps, reunite, how the river diverts itself around fallen trees and other debris, how these "intruders" can even cause the river to change its course altogether, and how tributaries influence the strength of the river's flow. So, the river is in a constant state of movement. Now picture a little water sprite popping up onto the surface of the water (and let's call that "birth"). It floats along, moving with the flow of the river, often being driven from one streamlet to another, swerving round rocks and obstacles, sometimes swimming against a diagonal current that takes it toward one bank then steering on an opposite pathway, often pushed back by the power of the current. Our sprite is often in contact with others on the river. Sustenance is available to this mythical creature from the river and its inhabitants. In turn, our water sprite excretes and drops fishbones into the stream thereby causing the chemical composition of the river to change. Over time our little sprite sinks under the surface and disappears from our view (let's call this "death") but continues to be part of the river by supplying nutrients as its body slowly disintegrates and is absorbed back into the riverbed. Thus, the sprite is part of the river, and the river is part of the sprite: both are part of the one system!

Without expanding this fanciful description of the life and death of one water sprite, we can use this analogy to explain "transitions" and "transformations." Like our water sprite, when human beings are born into a society, that is itself in constant change, they develop and change by the interaction of their own motive forces with the shifts and changes of the cultural environment in which they live. Hence, for a variety of reasons some of us are continually changing developmentally whereas others remain in the backwaters for lengthy periods. Some experience both shifts and calm periods because there will be "turning points" and obstacles to be surmounted throughout their life, and changes and shifts may affect only some aspects of the individual (what psychologists call "domain-specific" development). This also means that at times some aspects of our life course can cause us to regress in certain areas of development. Evans (2007) describes human progress through the life course as follows:

> When people move in social landscapes, how they perceive the horizons depends on where they stand. The horizons change strongly as they move, sometimes opening up, sometimes closing down. Where they go depends on the pathways they see, choose, stumble across, or clear for themselves, the terrain and elements they encounter.

What we are arguing is that it is useless to describe human transitions as "stages" because in our "movement" through the life course we are advancing, regressing, developing in some domains and not others; in a sense ever-becoming but never arriving! Thus, conceptualizing stages provides only a simplistic description of broad life-phases and does not allow us to grasp the complexities of different transitions, processes, and underlying, operational mechanisms. This has been stated some decades ago. In the 1970s, Riegel (1975) stressed that the primary goal of a developmental analysis is the study of change, not stasis! Yet only in the past few years have these ideas been incorporated into undergraduate textbooks (e.g., Thornton, 2008) and thereby found their way into mainstream psychology. We believe with Thelen and Baltes "that there are general principles of development: mechanisms and processes that hold true whatever the content domain" (Thelen & Baltes, 2003, p. 378), and that it is these processes and mechanisms we should analyze, instead of creating (normative) labels based on chronological age and mistake them for an explanation. In the following sections of this chapter this is the task we address by saying something about transitions to adulthood, describing systems theory as a framework for understanding the complex nature of these transitions, explaining various societal shifts, and introducing a simplified model of resources and challenges as one way of describing and analyzing human development.

Transitions from Adolescence and Adulthood

So, from our river analogy, adolescence is not a starting "point." Rather, it is itself a transition, with no clearly defined start or finish. A similar problem exists with the definition of adulthood. It is not possible to indicate the moment it starts, and with the vast and rapid changes occurring in our societies, which we discussed in the introductory chapter, it has become increasingly obsolete to use traditional "markers" of adulthood—such as leaving home, completing your education, finding a job, and starting a family of your own—to determine whether an individual has reached adulthood.

From a traditional psychological point of view, transitions mean changes in the body, in behavior, cognition, emotions, and skills that make individuals in one age group different from individuals in another age group. These changes can be on a larger or smaller scale, such as the transition to adulthood or the transition from Piaget's primary circular reactions to secondary circular reactions. Developmental psychologists have often chosen to describe these "transitions" as a succession of stages and substages, but nevertheless have always run into problems when trying to find definite starting points and end points of these stages. One reason for these problems is that development is often domain specific. For instance, we might agree that an individual can develop a mature adult physique, while at the same time not possessing the instrumental skills needed for living independently in a particular society. Furthermore, since behavior is multiply determined and assembled from the interactions of multiple subsystems, an "end goal," a "completed stage" is never achieved, because characteristics of both individuals and their contexts vary and change, and a "good fit" on one occasion may not be good on another (Ford & Lerner, 1992; Spencer et al., 2006). An individual's skills for independent living might be excellent under good economic conditions, but not remotely sufficient to cope with an economic crisis.

Sociologists look at the different sociocultural demands that individuals have to meet, and define a transition as a change in identities, roles, and statuses that are within the awareness of the individual and members of their in-group, their subcultures, and the culture of society. However, not all groups in society treat young people in the same way; there are different criteria by which teachers, parents, girl friends, advertising companies, employers, or the military determine the "adultness" of a person. The right to vote, marry, purchase alcohol, visit a nightclub, or be voted into a parliament are not all granted at the same age in a society, and most of these "adult" rights vary between countries. With this, sociologists run into a problem similar to psychologists in trying to define the end of adolescence and the start to adulthood. Historically in some cultures, there were "rites of passage" to mark the transition to adulthood, but modern societies have mainly discarded these (though there are still some religious traditions, such as First Communion, Conformation, and Bar Mitzvah, that remain as reminders of a time when rituals and ceremonies were of more transitional significance).

Thus, it is difficult to describe the changes that occur between adolescence and adulthood as "a transition from point A to B," because we cannot really define where "A" ends and "B" starts, since this differs between cultures and cohorts, between individuals, and even within individuals. What actually happens is a series of many minitransitions, some of which are reversible, some domain specific, and some more general: none of these occurs between two defined points.

So, adolescence and adulthood are not dichotomous. How the individual is seen depends, among other things, on the point of view of the observer, the task at hand, the personal circumstances of the individual, and the demands and support of the macrosystem. Rosenberger (2007) argued like this:

> What emerging adulthood is, what adulthood is, and how the two relate are moving targets in a constantly changing world. Emerging adulthood is a concept that allows us to think through rapidly changing, globalized lifestyles in richer countries in a new way. However, what

may be a global phenomenon of emerging adulthood will take different forms and meanings in relation to economic, political, and historical differences. . . . we should be open to elongated and ambiguous periods of emerging adulthood, that might even extend indefinitely, depending on the definition of adulthood and how quickly and in what way the definition changes in relation to cultural and historical logic. (Rosenberger, 2007, p. 95)

What we are really discussing are not transitions to adulthood, but a series of on-going transformations that occur, from the period labeled "adolescence" by stage theorists, through periods called "early adulthood," "midlife," and "old age," all the while experiencing changes and processes that enable us at any point in the life course to be defined concurrently as "a being," "a has-been," and "a becoming."

How do children eventually transform into adults? As we have argued above, we cannot answer that question by simply describing an array of stages they go through. Neither can we answer the question by looking at specific tasks they have to solve en route, as Havighurst (1972) proposed, because these tasks vary widely between individuals in different contexts and at different historical times. Nor can we decide when they have actually reached adulthood, because the definition of what characterizes "an adult" will vary in different societies at different times. "Assuming adult responsibilities" once historically meant that a man could be a hunter, endure pain, and survive in wild nature. Later, it meant being able to provide for a family. Now, in our modern society, it means being individually capable and responsible for our own life. However, even this might be changing. It would be a mistake to define "adult skills" as those our generation possesses, and then to measure the status of young people against this. Our grandmothers would have regarded the skill of preparing a family meal as absolutely basic for a fully adult woman. Today, with deep-frozen, ready-meals, this is a discretionary adult skill. On the other hand, with technology invading every part of our daily lives, the ability to handle electronic devices becomes more and more crucial for daily living—and young people may appear to be better equipped for this than present-day adults. So although some young people may not have acquired the skills that were traditionally seen as "markers of adulthood" (such as being economically independent), they do appear to possess certain survival skills in which the adult population of today may be less competent.

For all these reasons, we regard it as analytically fruitless to classify human beings as "children," "adolescents," or "adults" except for simple descriptive clarity, because the boundaries between these stages are vague, overlapping, and to a large extent arbitrary. To understand human development and change, we propose instead to analyze the processes and mechanisms that underlie developmental change in general. What is it that makes us change, and how does change occur—on the microlevel of the here and now, and on an ontogenetic level across the life span? Here we take and adapt a dynamic systems framework in analyzing these processes and mechanisms of human change.

A Systemic Perspective

What makes a systemic perspective different from traditional views of development is that it abandons the idea of simple, unidirectional and linear processes of cause and effect in explaining change. Instead, it sees nature as an open system that both consists of, and belongs to, a number of other open systems; and as human beings, we are part of this natural configuration. Hence, just like our water sprite in its river, the individual and the environment are not two entities separate from each other, but together form an open system (a point of view already offered by Vygotsky in 1930).

An open system does not have boundaries; it is embedded in larger systems and is in constant exchange with them. For example, from a systemic point of view, we would dismiss the question of whether it is "nature or nurture" that influences human development as a wrongly posed question. We do not regard "nature" and "nurture" as separate components: they are, as indeed is the developing individual himself or herself, part of the same system. Nor would it be correct to say that nature and nurture "interact"; that would be similar to describing your health as an interaction between heart and body. Individuals cannot interact with an environment of which they are integral elements (Thelen & Smith, 2006). Since this may be seen as an unorthodox way of thinking, we will clarify this idea by way of an illustration.

Consider, for example, that you are approaching a tray of apples in a fruit shop. Are they a part of you, or are they a part of your immediate and current environment? (The answer may not be as easy as you might at first consider.) If you are thinking of these apples, they are already "in your mind." When you see the apples lying in front of you, perceiving them, they have an impact on your perceptual system (and most likely on your digestive hormones). Now, you touch the apples, then choose one and buy it. Is the apple more certainly a part of you now than it was before? Or will it be when first you smell it, bite it, taste it, chew it, digest it? Then, how long will it be part of you? For as long as it remains within your digestive system or will it still be when pieces of it have left your body and are remitted (together with your body fluids) back to nature and transformed into other substances? What we want to demonstrate with this simple, yet complex, example is that there is no definitive answer as to when exactly the apple is part of you or when you are part of the apple.

In contrast to closed systems, which have no input from outside, so that their elements can maintain a stable relationship with each other (like water in a hermetically sealed bottle at constant temperature), open systems exchange matter and energy with other systems. Thus, they are never stable, but always in a dynamic flow. Hence even an apparently inactive adolescent lingering on the sofa is going through changes—hormones circulate in his or her body influencing mood, sounds are heard, thoughts are reflected on, the digestive system works, cells are renewed, beer and popcorn might enter the system, perspiration occurs, a nagging parent needs to be fended off . . . and all this is just a small part of his or her overall, continuous development.

Each system consists of many heterogeneous elements—such as molecules in body tissues, cells in a body, the body's physiological composition and anatomical make-up, individuals in a dyad or in society and in historical time. Each of these elements has certain degrees of freedom, which means it has different possibilities to "behave." Neurons may fire or not, action potentials can be transmitted or inhibited at synapses, eyes may be open or closed, an arm can be flexed or straightened, and moved in all directions, objects can be big or small, heavy or light, within reach or beyond reach and so on. Imagine what a complicated action it is to see an object, then reach out and grip it! This needs the organization and coordination of all these elements and is possible only if the degrees of freedom of each of the elements are considerably limited. Otherwise human movements would be chaotic, haphazard, and unpredictable. Compared to the full possible range of arm movements, there are only a few restricted types of movement that will lead to a seemingly simple skill such as successfully gripping an object. How much more difficult is it to master tasks that involve many more elements and different systems, such as learning the "adult skills" of planning ahead, managing time, and assuming responsibilities?

This process of "self-organization" in open systems means that the interactions of their elements lead to the spontaneous emergence of order within the system, because elements inhibit each others' degrees of freedom. The resulting patterns themselves are not static, but can undergo further changes in space and time. If the elements of the system interact repeatedly to reach a particular goal, they coordinate spontaneously and form a novel system. More or less erratic hand movements are, over time, organized into a goal directed grip, and young people through puberty will eventually learn to cope with their newly elongated limbs and changed body proportions and move gracefully again without needing to be taught. The ability to self-organize is essential for successful adaptation to changing circumstances (Guastello, 2002) (Box 4.1).

Apart from being complex and consisting of highly heterogeneous elements, open systems have another quality: they exist far from a so-called "equilibrium." A system is said to be at "equilibrium" when the energy and

---

BOX 4.1   Glossary

Degrees of freedom: The ways every element in a system can behave, before it becomes part of the system, when it will then be influenced and restricted by other elements of that system.

You may know the expression "degrees of freedom" from statistics: to achieve a given mean for a group of N observations, the first observations can take any value you like, but the last one needs to have the exact value needed to attain this mean. This is why the degrees of freedom in this case will always be $N - 1$.

As another example, imagine a blank sheet of SUDOKU, where you can choose freely where within the $9 \times 9 = 81$ cells you are going to place your first number. Once you have placed the first number, however, the degrees of freedom of where to place the second number are largely reduced, as the rules of the game do not allow you to place the same number into the same quadrant, column, or row as the first one. Each time you enter a new number, the degrees of freedom to enter the next will be reduced, until there is only one cell left in which to enter the last number. Degrees of freedom can describe the different ways an element can move, chemically react, formally fit, sound, or behave when it is not yet restricted by other elements in the same system.

To take an everyday example: You are invited to a magnificent dinner buffet, and to start with you have a choice between more than 50 dishes. However, as the evening goes on, the increasing fullness of your stomach and the choices of other guests will reduce your degrees of freedom of what to sample next considerably.

Cascading constraints: Once the degrees of freedom of elements in a system have been reduced, the system becomes relatively stable. When this system now starts to interact with other systems, it is more likely to do so in ways that fit its relatively stable organization rather than in others. This means it will not have complete freedom in its behavioral pattern—a chain of constraints has started.

Even though in the beginning it might have been genes and macroculture that formed the constraints of human action, each additional developmental step will continue to influence the formation of the next one. For example, during personality development, beliefs, appraisals, anxieties, and vulnerabilities emerging in early social interactions will form the baseline from which to approach new social encounters and influence them (Lewis, 1997).

Thus, psychomotor, social, emotional, and cognitive developmental pathways tend to be narrowed down and become increasingly inflexible—even though the original constraints may no longer be present.

Self-organization: The many elements within a system interact and thereby influence the degrees of freedom of other elements within the system. Eventually, order emerges from initial chaos, when all elements interact with each other in a relatively stable way. Self-organization means the spontaneous creation of coherent form within a system of interacting elements.

Picture a lecture room, and hundreds of students streaming into it, moving in different directions across the room. There are initially many degrees of freedom as to where they could sit down. However, each time a student takes a place, the degrees of freedom to choose a free seat will be reduced for the other students. After a while, all students are seated in their places and order has emerged within the lecture room. Similarly, when a couple move in together for the first time, they have many degrees of freedom as to who takes on particular household tasks. After a while, there are certain tasks that are more often performed by one or the other. Thus, a stable pattern emerges of who does what within this joint household.

Attractor state: A condition, shape, or place to which a system tends to be drawn, and energy, effort, or a significant change of circumstances would be needed to make the system move away from it. For example, a ball tends to roll downhill, a habit tends to be repeated, the pattern of established personal interactions is difficult to change, cultural values tend to outlive their functionality, alcoholism is difficult to cure, and association is easier than accommodation. The ultimate attractor state for any system is to reach equilibrium, where no input from outside is needed to maintain order in that system; however, in a biological system, this state is never fully attained.

(Continued)

BOX 4.1 (Cont'd)

Equilibrium: A state in which the elements of a system have found a perfect balance with each other, so that no element changes further and all are in homeostasis. Dynamic systems strive to reach the point of equilibrium, at which no input from outside is needed to maintain all its elements in balance. However, because there will always be an input from outside in biological systems, equilibrium will never be fully achieved or will be quickly disturbed by influences that always penetrate an open system. For instance, you might find moments at which you are completely at ease with yourself and the world around you, but these moments seldom last for long: you will feel hunger pangs, be disturbed by a telephone call, feel the urge to go to the toilet, have a sudden worrying thought—and that balanced state is gone again.

Nonlinear relationships: This is best understood as the opposite of linear relationships! A linear relationship exists when one variable in the equation causes the other variable to increase or decrease proportionally. For example, every calorie you eat will increase you weight a certain amount. Each year you additionally spend within the educational system is likely to increase your salary by a certain amount. The more you party, the less time you have for studying.

But nonlinear relationships do not work in such a straightforward way. First, there are relationships that work according to the all-or-nothing principle: e.g., the synapses of the central nervous system. An impulse may travel along your receptors, but it might not be strong enough to cause the synapse to fire. If the impulse is doubled or tripled, it may still not have any effect. But then, when it reaches the required threshold, it will cause your synapse to fire—though increasing it thereafter, it will not cause the synapse to fire more powerfully. It's an either/or condition.

Second, some other relationships are curvilinear. That means a little input leads to nothing, but too much input equally leads to nothing. A classic example of this is the Yerkes–Dodson Law: if you are not motivated at all, or if you are overmotivated to solve a complex task, you don't succeed particularly well—the optimal level of motivation in this case would be a medium level of motivation.

Many cause–effect relationships in real life are nonlinear. Just think of a problem you have been contemplating for a long time, and the time spent thinking does not seem to bring you any nearer to a solution.

Then, suddenly, often when you are completely relaxed and hardly think-ing about the problem, the solution appears as if by magic (this is also known as 'the Aha-effect!'). Apart from being an example of a nonlinear relationship between time of thinking and solution, this is also an exam-ple of spontaneous self-organization of a system: when elements are allowed to interact freely, they will self-organize into a pattern.

momentum of the system are uniformly distributed and there is no flow from one region to the other, as, for example, when salt is completely dissolved in water (Thelen & Smith, 1998). This "equilibrium" can be thought of as an "attractor" state, a stable place at which the system tends to settle or get stuck, and where least energy is used. However, though living systems "strive" to find homeostasis, they never achieve or stay in complete equilibrium, because they interact all the time with surrounding elements, which disturb the order and force the system to reorganize. Therefore, if a system receives sufficient input, it will move away from its attractor state and new ordered structures may spontaneously appear that were not formerly apparent: development has occurred.

This is why in human development there are often long periods in which seemingly nothing happens. Parents have been driven to despair by endlessly nagging their teenage children to get up in the morning in time for school: staying in bed is obviously a very stable attractor state in the teenage years. For most people, however, sleeping patterns change along the way to adulthood: the system is reorganized and finds a quite different attractor state. It is called developing a work-commitment!

Developmental changes are difficult to predict, because open systems are nonlinear systems. What does that mean? A linear relationship is, for example, number and weight: two spoons of sugar weigh exactly double one spoon of sugar. But an adolescent, who has passed two of the so-called "markers of adulthood" (e.g., has a job and a girlfriend) is not twice as adult than another adolescent who has achieved only one of these "markers"; and two nagging parents are not necessarily twice as effective in getting their teenager out of bed as one.

These are examples of nonlinear relationships: elements do not change proportionally with the variables that define them—the values of all the defining variables do not simply sum up or multiply. Because of this non-linearity, minimal change in one of the elements of a system can lead to abrupt shifts in the state of the system, much in the same way as the famous last drop that makes the glass overflow or the straw that is supposed to break the camel's back!

During these shifts, the system temporarily loses its ability to maintain its order and thereby loses dynamic stability, but can, after going through a period of "confusion," gain it again on a different level. A perfectly well-adapted teenager might start to act seemingly erratically, changing his or her behavior from day to day (or even from minute to minute) in a range from truculent aggression to complete cooperation (e.g., Coleman & Hendry, 1999), and then, within a short time, "suddenly" settling down to behave in a consistent and amicable way.

However, over time the more order that has accumulated through self-organization of the system, the more input is usually needed to shift its direction. Once a system has created an order of patterns through self-organization, a precedent for the direction of further change is created—and certain other pathways are more or less excluded. Lewis (2000) calls this phenomenon "cascading constraints," because it constrains possibilities for the system's future pathways: once stem cells have been arranged to form a hand, they can no longer transform into another body part, and once a young person has decided on a particular career, has taken out a large mortgage to buy a house, or has become pregnant, the range of further lifestyle options is somewhat restricted. Like the degrees of freedom of each single element, the number of possible attractor states is eventually reduced by the increasing order and complexity of the interactions of the dynamic system. Though behavior emerges in the moment, the effects of each behavioral decision accumulate over longer time scales, as each change sets the stage for future changes, so that past behavior still has an influence on present behavior (Spencer et al., 2006). This is not only true for single individuals, who forge their particular and varied paths through life each time they make a decision. Because our lives are linked to others, traces of contemporary and former generations' life choices are woven into the system in which our own behavior emerges. Current historical events shape, to some extent, the conditions under which a young person enters adulthood, but so too do decisions that have been taken by the parents and grandparents long before the individual was born. Their choices about where to live, what kind of family to form, and what employment to seek still affect descendant generations (Elder, 1997).

Thus, we can see here other examples of self-organization and shift from macrolevels to microlevels of a society. The economic base of a society, its traditional values system, the distribution of hegemonic power and social status within it, and individual characteristics all interact and lead to the self-organization of relatively stable roles for different members in that society, for example, gender roles or the norms and expectations directed toward different age groups. Bynner (2005) uses the concept of individual pathways to explain how they link one "status passage" to the next:

> Such biographical pathways are longitudinal in the sense that each step along them is conditioned by the steps taken previously, by the personal, financial, social and cultural resources to which the growing individual has access, and by the social and institutional contexts through which the individual moves. (Bynner, 2005, p. 379)

The social system itself is never completely stable; there are always exceptions and rebels, the status quo will always be questioned, so that the system is continuously in a state of flux and changing in concert with the elements within it. Leaving this attractor state would lead to instability and crisis, which is unsettling for individuals, whose resistance to change and nostalgic yearnings about "keeping to the old ways" add to the system remaining in a particular attractor state for a lengthy time period, in spite of dynamic currents to create disequilibrium. It needs a powerful force (such as an industrial, technological, or political revolution) to get a society out of balance and eventually change toward a new attractor state.

In summary, from a systemic perspective human development is seen as the interplay of various elements in an open system, which self-organizes and is relatively stable from time-to-time, but ever so often is brought into imbalance and has to reorganize itself on a different, more complex level.

Resources and Challenges

So in what ways can dynamic system theory help us to understand human transformations from child to adult (and beyond)? We will utilize our simplified theoretical framework of developmental change (Hendry & Kloep, 2002) to illustrate this.

At the outset, we want to take a closer look at the resources for development that are available to human beings. All healthy children are born with a certain range and level of fairly similar resources that help them to develop into adult human beings (no one has yet been reported as having developed into a frog Prince!) and to cope with life's challenges. Importantly, these resources will change and alter over the life course. Furthermore, all babies get bigger, all have a predisposition to learn to walk and speak a language, to see, to hear and to smell, to learn new things, and to feel varying emotions.

Consequently, Indian and Russian, British and Maori neonates, and those in rich and poor families, behave in much the same way.

Accepting these similarities, we are also very different from each other from the day we are born, and even as fetuses in the womb. Many of our resources are innate, such as certain reflexes. Others are learned, since learning starts in the first seconds of life and will go on until death. Still others are structurally determined, such as nationality or social class. Just as certain potential resources exist for every individual from the very first moments of life in the womb, so too does the inequality in their distribution among individuals. Furthermore, some resources are more "personal" to the individual (such as intelligence) and some are more societal. Indeed they can potentially include all the groups from family, school, clubs, peers, to the local community itself that may have a function of intermediary between the individual and society (e.g., Shucksmith & Hendry, 1998; Small, & Supple, 2001), and which create different opportunities, such as whether education is available and affordable, the employment situation, climate, laws, health system, and cultural traditions. Hence, they encompass conditions of the individual's micro-, meso-, and macrosystems (Bronfenbrenner, 1979) and they are all potential resources.

The idea of a "resource system" to describe an individual's potential to cope with various challenges has also appeared in sociological literature. Côté (1996) uses the concept of "identity capital" (which consists of sociological assets, such as educational level, and psychological resources, such as critical thinking abilities) to describe the resources an individual possesses to deal with the demands of modern living and development throughout the life course. The number and kind of resources can vary at any moment in time and over the lifespan. New resources are added, others disappear, some characteristics become resources, and some lose their resourceful quality.

None of the variables within these different categories should be seen in isolation from the others, rather they should be regarded as highly interactive. Biological and sociostructural variables, for example, interact with acquired skills, and together form the basis of self-efficacy, which in turn enhances the learning of new skills. Consider for a moment a female child who is, because of her gender (i.e., structural resource), not allowed to play boisterously with her peers. She may not develop the skills of self-defense (i.e., skills resource), and thus be at higher risk of becoming an assault victim, which in turn, might have an impact on her self-efficacy and health resources. Low self-efficacy can lead to shyness, fewer social contacts, and thus to fewer social resources, and so on.

To take a positive example, a child born with a musical talent might find an adult who is willing to further this gift. Having a mentor and a skill that is admired by peers and potential romantic partners is a good prerequisite to stay out of "trouble" by not having to impress peers with more risky, perhaps delinquent behaviors. All this can strengthen self-esteem and lead to further social contacts and new associated skills.

Now this view of individual resources would not be a systemic one if we regarded the resource system as static and closed. Of course, this is not the case. First, as already mentioned, potential resources interact with each other so that they can enhance and/or inhibit each other. For example, physical attractiveness can be a resource in many social contexts and enhance self-esteem. However, it can also inhibit the learning of social skills—the individual relying solely on good looks to be accepted by peers. Or being a talented soccer player can enhance your health and fitness and gain peer approval, yet it can also lead to sports injuries and fiercely competitive attitudes to others—and in some young people, being an active sports participant during adolescence even predicts heavy alcohol use in young adulthood (Peck, Vida, & Eccles, 2008).

Second, the resource system participates in other open systems. So whereas in some situations being a creative, critical thinker could bring you a King's sponsorship, in other circumstances it could lead you to the hangman's noose! Or to take a more contemporary example, being a creative and critical thinker could win you a doctoral scholarship, in other contexts it could bring you the boss's disapproval and dismissal. Social embeddedness in a community and strong links with your family can be a powerful resource in meeting various challenges, but it can turn into a disadvantage when it prevents a young person from moving away to pursue a university education or a career (Henderson et al., 2007). A plethora of material resources can buy better food, healthier housing, and better health care, as we can observe in the richer countries of the world. It also enhances the probability for obesity, alcohol and drug dependency, and inactivity, as the same statistics show (World health Organization, 2008). Thus, potential resources can become disadvantageous while potential disadvantages can become beneficial, depending on the interaction with other elements in the participating systems.

Third, some resources that are beneficial in the short term can become potentially harmful or even highly risky in the longer term. The increasing availability of unskilled, temporary part-time work in Western societies does give young people work experience and a wage. However, if they continue to rely on the same or similar jobs for some years into the future it may constrain their opportunities to gain complete freedom from their parents, because these wages are too low and too unpredictable to allow for independent living (Martín, 2002). Or even more dramatically, drugs prescribed to offset depression may in the long term lead to drug dependency.

Hence, we cannot define what a resource actually is—or what might become one—without considering it in interaction with the challenges the individual will meet. Likewise, we would not know whether to put salt or sugar into a dish without knowing what kind of food the dish contained! For this reason, it is advantageous for individuals to build up a whole range of different skills in various domains, as it is impossible to predict what kinds of challenges they are going to face across the life span, and which of these skills might become a valuable resource one day.

This is particularly relevant because challenges are defined by resources, and vice versa. Only by knowing an individual's resources can we decide whether a particular task is a challenge, and only by knowing a particular task can we decide if an individual has the resources to deal with it. What we are trying to say here is that it is impossible to view resources without looking at challenges at the same time: the two are inexorably linked, in fact they are part of the same open system, and what we are really analyzing is not resources on the one hand and challenges on the other, but the relationship between the two.

To illustrate this further, no potential resource is a resource in isolation. For example, is it a challenge for young people to manage their own apartment? It can well be, if they never had to do any housekeeping before. But it is no more than a routine task for those who have previously participated in household tasks in their parental home. Similarly, having a lot of money can most certainly be a resource, if the challenge is of a nature that can be solved with money (for example, hiring a cleaner, if the individual lacks cleaning skills). However, money can also be completely irrelevant in other situations (e.g., when sitting for an examination) or even a disadvantage (e.g., looking at an array of expensive Belgian chocolates while trying to maintain a healthy diet). Actually, money can be changed from a potential resource into a challenge, if there is a lack of economic planning skills (as is often observed in lotto millionaires, for whom sudden riches can be more than they can handle).

Similarly, whenever young people's risk behaviors and lifestyle choices are regressed on a series of potential predictors in psychological research, "education" emerges as a strong protective factor (Jessor, 2008). This kind of research, however, springs not only from a relatively static cause-and-effect view of the world, it is also biased with a normative definition of what constitutes a "healthy outcome," thereby ignoring all the microprocesses that become invisible in a regression model and/or lost in the error variance. It might be true that a higher level of education is correlated with less risky behavior, but it is also true that in many peer cultures today, academic ability and an aptitude for studying are regarded as "uncool" and make the "nerd" vulnerable to bullying and social exclusion. That might effectively stop her or him from participating in drinking sprees—but is it really a healthy outcome? Furthermore, what is it that seems to be "protective" about education? Is it the academic skills achieved, is it the teachers' supervision that keeps young people off the street, is it the better work prospects that come along with better grades, or is it enhanced self-esteem? Again, we need to know the processes and mechanisms that function to protect some young people from engaging in certain risk behaviors. Simply forcing thousands of disengaged, alienated teenagers to attend two more years of compulsory schooling, as is currently being debated in the UK, seems unlikely to solve anything. Education might be a resource for many young people in many contexts, but being a good statistical predictor does not necessarily make it a panacea. It is the obvious limitations of this kind of research that have led dynamic system theorists to urge abandoning variable centered studies in favor of person-centered research (Valsiner, 1997).

Thus, although the task determines what a resource is, the number and kind of potential resources within an individual's resource system determine whether the particular task the individual meets turns out to be a routine chore, a challenge, or a risk. Elder (1986, 1987), for example, has shown that during the Great Depression in the United States, being called up for military service had a differential impact on young men depending on when in their life course it happened. It had positive effects on younger men, who had just left high school, because it saved them from unemployment and gave them the opportunity to learn entrepreneurial skills, which were important for their future careers. Nevertheless, the same military service had negative effects on older men, because it disrupted their careers and their families.

In other cases, stressors that disrupt the continuity of your life can act as "catalysts for change" (Fiske & Chiriboga, 1991). Therefore, a certain amount of stress can be regarded positively from a developmental point of view, because it can lead to the acquisition of new skills (Aldwin, 1992). Hence, a task can be a clearly positive experience, or it may contain negative elements that, nevertheless, lead to growth. For example, having a physical handicap has, for some people, been the antecedent to enormous personal growth, whereas something as apparently desirable as getting a promotion can be disastrous for a person who lacks the managerial skills to cope with new responsibilities. Gottlieb, Still, and Newby-Clark (2007), in analyzing the impact of life events on development in emerging adulthood, concluded that whereas development could be limited only by negative experiences, growth could be stimulated by all kinds of life events, ranging from those perceived as very undesirable to those perceived as very desirable.

As a systemic framework, the resources-challenge model is a useful, simplified tool for analyzing the changing life courses of individuals in changing societies by taking into account the ways different individuals encounter different experiential challenges by utilizing a varying set of resources in meeting these and by explaining how challenges, resources, and risks are all dynamically linked across the life course. It can also provide insights into how some individuals develop and others "stagnate" either by choice of lifestyle or through lack of relevant challenges and resources.

Development and Change

Each time an individual meets a challenge, the system of challenges and resources becomes unbalanced, as the individual is forced to adapt his or her resources to meet this particular challenge. This adaptation can be short-lived if the resources easily match the challenge, as in dealing with routine tasks. On the other hand, it can be a long, anxiety-provoking process when the challenge is significant (or when there are several challenges encountered at the same time; see Coleman, & Hendry, 1999) and matching resources are not easily available. If the individual is eventually able to solve the task, his or her resources are transformed and increased, and it will be easier to cope with similar challenges in the future. In other words, the individual has changed, and development has occurred.

What this means is that there need to be challenges for development to occur—or to use the terminology of dynamic systems theory, the system needs an input to become unbalanced and to reorganize on a more complex level. The idea of a "conflict" that triggers change is actually not new within developmental psychology; we can find it, for example, in the notion of equilibration in Piaget's theory, in the necessity of crises in Erikson's stage theory, and in Riegel's (1979) dialectical psychology.

If we leave the theoretical terminology for a moment and turn to some real life examples, we can easily see how young students, starting for the first time at a university, see themselves confronted with a whole range of new challenges. To leave home, find new friends, adjust to a different way of teaching and learning, manage their own economy, and spend their evenings unfettered by parents are all new experiences that tax their resource systems and bring them out of equilibrium. There will be a time of confusion, during which all elements of the system—existing resources and existing challenges (which vary with the history of the individual) as well as emerging challenges and emerging resources (which vary with the new environment, such as support systems of the university, subject-specific demands, peer group climate, housing conditions, etc.) to interact and reorganize themselves into a new system with a new attractor point: a competent student is evolving from the confused freshman. However, when the time comes, this system will be shaken up again, and the student will have to reorganize into an employee!

Meeting a challenge that "disturbs" the system can be both exciting and anxiety provoking. Every organism has processes by which it defends itself against, overcomes, or adapts to such perturbations (Ford & Lerner, 1992), and each response to such a disruption means simultaneously losing an existing secure position (i.e., development as risk) and an increase in possibilities (i.e., development as progress). This creates feelings of both hope and insecurity in the individual (Dreher, 2007), and explains why it is sometimes more comfortable to try to avoid further challenges and to choose "the way of least resistance" (in systemic terms: to keep to the old attractor state). Subjectively this is a comfortable state, but it does not offer a great deal of potential development. Hendry and Kloep (2002) have chosen to call this situation "contented stagnation." An example of this can be a young person who objectively has the resources (e.g., money, skills, available housing) to leave the parental home, but finds it much cheaper and more comfortable to stay and have his meals cooked, his room cleaned, and his laundry washed. This is a reasonable adaptation to the existing circumstances, but it does not offer him the chance to learn the skills of independent living.

Conversely, when an individual does not have the resources to seek out further challenges, this also prevents development because the individual just maintains the status quo and is not able to change. Hendry and Kloep (2002) have called this "unhappy stagnation" because it is imposed, not chosen. An example could be a young girl who had poor grades in school and is unable to find work locally, yet wants to have her own apartment. However, she ends up without education or employment and unable to leave her parental home as she hoped.

To summarize, human change comes about by a systemic interaction of different resources and challenges, and not simply by the passing of time. Every new challenge causes the system to change. This can consist of a reorganizing of the system and a major transformation or of avoiding challenges and keeping the system more or less near to equilibrium. Only the first of these options leads to what we would term "development."

Shifts

The processes and mechanisms of change are the same for all humans independent of culture, cohort, and age; yet what makes them so different across these parameters are life experiences. On the one hand, all normal babies develop into adults, and eventually they grow old and die. On the other hand, some of them will become parents and some will not; some of them will be outstanding in intellectual pursuits and others will hardly learn to read or write. Some will spend most of their adult lives in prison, others will live in mansions, and still others will live in a tin hut in the forest or in an urban slum.

In addition, each young person will have unique experiences from the very first day of birth. A second child in a family is actually not living in the same environment as its older sibling, even if it might appear so superficially. First, an older brother or sister exists. Second, the parents are some years older, more experienced, and, possibly, in a different phase of their life; friends and relatives do not react in the same way to the arrival of each new child; there are different peers to interact with in the nursery school, and so on. In other words, everyday life is different in many small aspects, which collectively and interactively lead to a different life course. The different challenges individuals meet across their life span play a significant role in human diversity in development.

If we look at teenagers across the world, we see that what happens to their bodies during puberty is similar no matter where and when they live. Their hormonal system starts to change, which causes them to develop their primary and secondary sex characteristics, and they eventually reach a state of adult maturity. There is some variability as to when exactly they have their menarche or first nocturnal emission, but it will, with great certainty, happen within the second decade of their life, given that they are healthy and well nourished. Thus, it is important to note that even for a biological shift such as puberty we have to take context variables into account.

In other words, there are certain changes in life that will happen to all humans relatively independently of the influences of their physical and cultural environment. These changes are "maturational shifts" caused mainly by normal biological mechanisms, such as puberty, the menopause, and ageing. Even if there are certain variations in the onset and duration of these maturational changes between individuals within the same culture, and between groups in different cultures, the processes involved, and the biological outcomes, are similar for all human beings. These shifts are expected and experienced by everyone. They are nevertheless a challenge, because the individual will have to cope with and adjust to them psychosocially. However, the ability to prepare for them and the presence of older role models make them relatively easy to face. It is maturational shifts that account for the similarity in human development throughout the world, and which led some earlier psychologists to believe that all development follows a given, genetically determined pattern.

Human beings within one cultural setting are closely similar. Hence, the people in individualistic societies of rich Western nations differ significantly from the collective cultures of the developing countries. However, even within the same culture, there are subcultural differences (i.e., men compared to women, working classes compared to middle and upper classes, different religious groups, youth subcultures, and regional variations). For example, in the United States, differences have been observed as to when and why young people from varying cultural backgrounds leave home. Catholics leave home later than all other groups, whereas fundamentalist Protestants leave home at a fairly early age for marriage, and liberal Protestants do so to go to college (Goldscheider & Goldscheider, 1994).

As we have previously commented, cultures change over time: ancient Britain was different from modern Britain, and being a teenager in the 1970s posed different challenges than those facing an adolescent today. Thus, although all members of all cultures share the same maturational shifts, one significant set of influences that causes differences between cultures is the developmental transitions we call "normative-social shifts," and to a certain degree those we call "quasinormative shifts."

Normative shifts are changes in our life that are prescribed by law for all members of certain well-defined groups. Within a country, these could be for, example, starting school, achieving adult legal status, and retiring from paid employment. These shifts occur in the lives of almost all members of a particular culture at given times in their life. Thus, they are predictable, expected, and shared with peers. Age-graded procedures like these are to be found in every society, though their enforcement varies considerably by culture.

Quasi-normative shifts are experiences which are not prescribed to the same degree, but common and socially expected to occur within a certain age range in a given culture. Examples for these shifts are leaving the parental home, age at first marriage, getting a first job, parenthood, and other cultural symbols like age-related clothes fashions, hair style and musical interests. Both normative and quasinormative shifts account for similarities between members within certain cultural groups, and for differences between cultural groups; and these normative and quasi-normative shifts are not static within a culture or subculture. Since cultures themselves are open systems, expectations vary concurrently with changes in the cultural system. Hence, expectations about childhood, adolescence, and young adulthood continuously change over the course of history, between societies and within societies.

Moreover, there is a range of nonnormative shifts awaiting individuals across their life course. Nonnormative shifts are changes that do not occur for everyone, but only for some, perhaps for very few individuals. The number of possible nonnormative shifts that can occur across the life course is almost infinite, though examples could include a serious accident or injury, but also moving to a foreign country or a radical career change. These shifts can be developmental "turning points" (or "turning processes"), and they can have enduring consequences by affecting subsequent events through a process of cumulative advantages or disadvantages ("cascading constraints," in the language of dynamic system theory). However, we should keep in mind that many of these "transitions" do, in reality, consist of multiphasic processes of relatively long duration. They frequently comprise a succession of several "points of choice," and not single, short-lived events (Elder, 1998). Thus, these shifts present the individual with a host of challenges, and each of these can be dealt with more or less successfully.

To sum up, we argue that it is these individual processes of change, acting in concert with all other elements of the wider system, that explain human development rather than the simple passing of time. We develop by meeting and coping with a myriad of challenges from day to day—and not by moving through age-bound stages.

Summary: A New Way of Analyzing Transitions to Adulthood

In this chapter we have discussed the difficulties inherent in defining the notions of "adolescence," "adulthood," and, as a consequence, "transitions," and argued that trying to describe human development by these vague, ill-defined concepts does not add to our understanding of what causes human change across the lifespan. Therefore, by way of an analogy about a river and a river sprite, we proposed an alternative systemic view, that seeks to analyze the processes and mechanisms that underlie human transformations, by considering the resources and challenges involved in development across the life span. We regard the individual as an open system, embedded in a diversity of microsystems and macrosystems, which in turn influence the kind and number of challenges met. Hence, the mechanisms involved in meeting normative and quasinormative shifts do not vary between cultures and historic cohorts, whereas cultural conditions and their associated challenges do. For this reason, the individual pathways from childhood to adulthood vary enormously. For some children, there are nonnormative shifts that cause them to grow up very quickly, whereas for others, different nonnormative shifts have prolonged their period of "transition" to more than a decade. Some are forced by societal conditions to shorten or prolong this period, whereas others have some choice in the pace of their transition, depending on their resources. In subsequent chapters we will utilize this theoretical perspective and way of thinking to interpret the varying pathways of transformation that exist for young people in culturally different societies throughout the world.

5

Lifestyles in Emerging Adulthood: Who Needs Stages Anyway?

Leo B. Hendry and Marion Kloep

Introduction: Transitions, Resources, and Challenges

In today's rapidly changing world, traditional developmental tasks such as gaining independence from parents, making personal living arrangements, orienting to a career, and developing new sets of relationships with parents, peers, and romantic partners are differently ordered, and these present young people with significant challenges in gaining adult status, as Tanner and Arnett correctly point out. However, modern theorists have claimed that emerging adulthood is not a universal stage, but depends on the cultural—and subcultural—contexts in which young people develop and the social institutions they encounter (e.g., Heinz & Marshall, 2003; Bynner, 2005; Reitzle, 2006). Even Arnett and Tanner acknowledge that the time of life they call emerging adulthood is extremely heterogeneous. Describing diversity, however, is not enough. There is a need for a more thorough examination of the multivarious circumstances of developmental transitions than have been presented in Tanner and Arnett's picture of the emerging adult (see Chapter 2). There are stressful issues in early adulthood, especially for those young people who are still emerging, not by choice, but because they *lack* choice. They are restricted by their lack of social, relational, and/or occupational opportunities and skills. Hence, different trajectories from adolescence into early adulthood demonstrate a greater diversity of opportunities, risks, and well-being even in our Western cultures. On the one hand, individualization can lead to greater autonomy and an increasing number of life options. On the other hand, it can also be linked to a heightened risk of failure, insecurity, and stress (e.g., Parker et al., 1998). As Jones and Wallace (1992) and Bynner (2005) have pointed out, the choices in young adulthood are still dependent to a high degree on a range of structural social factors together with family and community bonds (see, e.g., Shucksmith & Hendry, 1998; Small & Supple, 2001).

Findings from studies of non-Western cultures and ethnic minorities suggest that generalizations about emerging adults do not capture the variations that exist within individuals and across cultures (Arnett, 2003; Nelson, Badger, & Wu, 2004; Cheah, & Nelson, 2004). As Lloyd et al. (2005) have observed, the largest generation of young people in history is now making the transition from childhood to adulthood, with 86% of this cohort, nearly 1.5 billion individuals, living in developing countries, experiencing very different lives from those of affluent Westerners:

> While some young people are engaged in wars and civil strife, others are voting for the first time. While some young people are accessing the Internet, others have never been to school. Thus, despite global changes that have led to a convergence of experiences among young people in certain domains of life, the experiences of many young people remain sharply divergent. (Lloyd, 2005, p. 580)

Therefore, in this chapter we will examine what influences young people's developmental pathways, and what makes them different from each other in different cultures and subcultures. To understand the changes that have occurred for many young people individually, we need to consider the changes that have occurred on the macrolevel of their societies as well as factors within their microsystems that influence their development (Bronfenbrenner, 1979). Alongside these theoretical descriptions we will use case studies to provide real-life examples encountered in our own research (see Boxes 5.1–5.7).

We start by considering the influences of macrosocial conditions, such as the prevailing economic system, on the roles of children, adolescents, and young adults, and how this is mediated by governmental and institutional policies that are in place in different countries. Then we go on to analyze how value systems (which are rooted in economic conditions) can continue to exert an influence on young peoples' transitions even when these conditions have changed. Finally, we take an in-depth look at how parents, influenced by all of

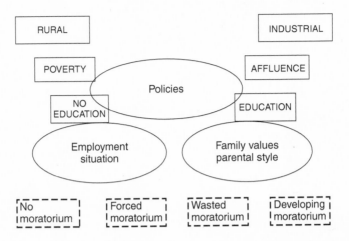

FIGURE 5-1

the above, go on to create microsystems for their sons and daughters that facilitate or prevent a smooth transition to adulthood.

An outline diagram of our analysis of the various systems implied in creating different pathways into adulthood is presented in Fig. 5.1. (Note that as true dynamic systems "fans," we have abstained from using arrows because we regard those interactions as multidirectional and multifunctional.)

The Economic System and Transitions to Adulthood

To examine the role of economic conditions on transitions to adulthood, we have taken Jensen's (1994, 2001) analysis of the "feminization of childhood," and expanded it by presenting a series of societal typologies, in an attempt to account for the changing roles, and consequently changing lives, of children in different economic conditions.

Agricultural Societies and Rurality

In predominantly rural societies, the economy is based on a large number of farming families. These families owe their existence to the land and its produce, and failure to harvest can end in economic ruin. Children in such a society are not only cheap labor, but most of all, they guarantee survival for the older and weaker members of their extended family. As an insurance for old age, they constitute an economic investment, and for that reason it is important to have many children (particularly in times of high child mortality), and to ensure many survive. Thus, both the children and their mother are valuable "possessions" for the farmer. They make it possible for him to survive, and for the rural society to function. Thus, it is important that there are strong families with many children, with traditions and laws to protect them. The children and wife retain the father's name, divorce is impossible or extremely difficult, and some societies allow for polygamy and encourage marriage between first cousins to keep material assets within the extended family. In addition, under hard living conditions there has to be a clear line of command: facing a hailstorm when the harvest has not yet been brought in needs strong leadership and does not leave time for democratic discussions. The patriarch of the family is not to be questioned.

Childhood does not exist—nor does adolescence or emerging adulthood: children join the work force as soon as they are able. We still find this economic system in rural areas in Africa, Latin America, and Asia, and, for example, in indigenous rural and poor urban communities in the Peruvian Andes, Guatemala, and Panama (Galambos & Martínez, 2007; Dries-Daffner, Hallman, Catino, & Berdichevsky, 2007; Flores, 2007). In developing countries, 81% of young men and 88% of young women in the age group 20–24 years are not in education, and enrollments in postsecondary schools in sub-Saharan countries, the former Soviet Asia, and South America have even declined over the past few years (Lloyd, 2005).

This way of life has been "self-organized" (to use dynamic systems language) as an adaptation to the economic conditions of these areas. In other words, values arose from economic needs and had an important function for the society in general. Its adaptive value became apparent, for instance, when the Chinese Government implemented a necessary "one-child" policy as seen from a strategic "population-control" point of view. They met extreme resistance, particularly in rural areas, a fact that in the urban capital was viewed as revisionist tendencies based on an old-fashioned, useless value system. In the rural areas, however, it soon became obvious that the values of nourishing the extended family were far from useless; single children saw themselves as unable to support their aging parents, who faced an old age in poverty (Shixun, 1994).

Although it makes sense to people living in predominantly rural societies to invest in children instead of education, and to keep strong links within an extended family with a patriarchal structure, from early in their history most countries had other forms of economic activities and thus associated, competing values and different lifestyles.

Mixed Economies

Historically many societies develop a mix of economic patterns: manufacture, trade, and service professions soon begin to appear alongside the farming industry, and urbanization takes place. For a minority of citizens, there is no longer the same need to possess a large family. Indeed, living conditions in the cities are too cramped to allow for extended families to live comfortably, and a large number of children can become an economic liability instead of an investment. However, for the stability of rural society *as a whole*, and particularly for the wealthy and powerful, the old lifestyle still has many advantages, and so they try to preserve it, using such devices as codifying laws, proclaiming certain values, and propagating particular religious doctrines. All sexual activities that do not lead to child bearing (homosexuality, premarital and extramarital sex, abortion, contraception) are outlawed, and virtues of family, obedience, and hard work are promoted. These measures are effective enough to prevent massive changes in society for some time.

However, the continuing rise of industrialization and the accompanying decrease of agricultural living lead to an ever increasing need for a more educated work force; and with the raising of educational standards it becomes increasingly difficult to direct the masses by indoctrination. They start to question laws and values, and begin to protest against traditions that no longer make sense to them. Intellectuals give rise to enlightenment movements, students riot, and people demand a reform of values and laws. Now a large number of educated people turn out to be dangerous for those who want to maintain the status quo and prevent societal change. This became obvious, for example, as recently as the middle of the twentieth century, when conservative forces in Nicaragua tried to stop an ongoing revolution by killing teachers, who had tried to develop the literacy of the rural population. The significance of education in affecting change is also well known to reformers. One famous slogan of revolutionaries from the late eighteenth century onward has been the following: *"If you want to make the poor people rise: Educate, agitate, organize!"*

These contradictory tendencies of conservatism and change also lead to an imbalance in the microsystems where different values coexist. Differing roles and transitions to adulthood depend on a variety of factors: whether young people live in a rural or urban context, what value system the family and community adhere to, and on the family's relative wealth. Thus, some will grow up quickly, assume adult responsibilities early, and endorse collectivist values, while not becoming totally independent of their parents for some time; others, dependent on their advantageous circumstances, are given a prolonged childhood, and even a period of adolescence, during which they are educated with the aim of becoming independent from their parents. This leads to them questioning the old values, rebelling against a patriarchal order, and striving toward more individualist goals.

This is the situation many countries outside the highly industrialised Western economies are in today. Less than 20% of Chinese young people get a college education (Nelson & Chen, 2007), yet access to good jobs is dependent on education. Those who enter the work force in their teens are overwhelmingly likely to work in rural, agricultural jobs. Urban–rural and socioeconomic differences are evident in the health problems facing China's adolescents: youths in some rural areas continue to face basic health problems such as lack of adequate nutrition, whereas wealthier urban youth are beginning to face "Western-type" health issues associated with obesity and smoking (Hannum & Jihong, 2005). In Peru, Guatemala, Panama, Belize, Costa Rica, Honduras, and Mexico some children are precipitated into adult responsibilities and start to work early, whereas urban adolescents from the upper classes in the same countries often study abroad and enjoy the full moratorium of emerging adulthood (Galambos & Martínez, 2007).

In Turkey, the divide between rural and urban areas reflects the division of family values as a function of the underlying economic conditions: rural people still see children as economic investments, and thus cling to traditions such as favoring sons over daughters and wishing to have many children. In contrast, people in urban areas have children for emotional/psychological reasons, and consequently tend to have fewer children and prefer daughters to sons, as they are considered more likely to repay the emotional investment in their socialization by offering parental care and concern (Ataca, Kagıtcıbası, & Diri, 2005).

Postmodern Societies

The macrosystem of any culture is embedded into a set of other systems, for example, a global relationship with other countries. The rapid development of high technology has led to an intensification of international competition, and to a rapidly increasing need for a highly qualified labor force. In a situation like this, it is no longer in the best interests of a society to have half its potentially intelligent population in domestic roles looking after a multitude of children that are no longer required economically. To release women from the home for education and into the work force, the (welfare) state now takes over some previous domestic tasks, in particular, the protection and education of children and the care of the elderly. Instead of former collective production, family members today share only collective consumption (Buchmann, 1989).

This has tremendous consequences for women and young people in wealthy societies. With children no longer needed as an insurance against old age, there are now no *economic* reasons for their existence. On the contrary, it has become extremely expensive to raise children, if lost wages and child-care expenses are taken into account. As a consequence, birth rates have plummeted in the highly industrialized countries throughout the past five decades, and it is a widely replicated finding almost everywhere in the world that the longer education of girls subsequently reduces fertility rates, independent of the husband's education and social class (Weisner & Lowe, 2005). But that is not the only change. Having children is now a lifestyle choice. Kalle et al. (2000) describe the decision to have children as the "Porsche-option"—a choice between expensive consumer goods or a child. Men may be more often inclined to choose the former, so when they "give in" to their partner's wish to have children; they feel less obliged to assume the same level of responsibility. This had an impact on the macrosystem: children can now have their mother's name, divorce has been made relatively easy, cohabitation without legal formalities is possible, and an increasing number of children are born outside wedlock—actually, fertility is higher in countries such as Sweden, where women can give birth and provide for children without being married, than in countries where this is not the case, such as Italy (Jensen, 2001). Apart from decreasing birth rates, this economic and societal change has led to new roles for children and young people. If parents decide to procreate in spite of the economic costs, they do so for emotional reasons. Children now enter the family not as "co-workers," but as love objects, very much like highly valued pets! Parents, who are, in the main, wealthier than the previous generation, have the means to indulge their children with consumer goods, while having less time to spend with them. There is no longer the need for a patriarchal system to survive the severities of life, so values of obedience and authority have become less firm and less significant; and children—well schooled from early on—have the ability (and use it!) to question any parental attempts to impose their authority. So instead of a strictly hierarchical family structure there is now a democratic one, or even, in some cases, a situation of anarchy:

> In response to this increasing tyranny of childhood, bewildered and frustrated parents are looking for help. Their children, by the standards of virtually all known societies, behave like spoiled brats who cannot control their impulses, take responsibility for their actions, or empathize with others. (Côté, 2000, p. 89)

Being their children's best friends, parents have now limited influence on their children's choices of lifestyle (Côté, 2000), and, more often than not,

BOX 5. 1   "I Suppose I Baby Him" . . . Mother of a 22-Year-Old Student

He is still very much a child when he comes home. He is at the university at the moment, so he has a lot of independence and to be honest, he doesn't come home that often. In this respect I would consider him an adult, because he does all his own cooking, lives in his own house, and pays his own rent and bills, but I don't think he does his own washing, because when he comes home every 4 weeks or so he has two very big plastic bags full of washing, but then he is still young.

I suppose I baby him when he comes home, because I don't see him very often. I cook all his meals for him, do his washing, give him lifts to places he needs to go, and I suppose I just do everything for him.

I would say that I do treat him differently from when he was about 15 years old, but he is 22 years old now. Before he left for the university at 19 years of age, when he lived at home, I used to treat him as I think anyone would treat a teenager. I used to do a lot for him and I used to be very protective of him. Like when he used to go out I'd want to know where he was going, who he was with, and exactly what time he'd be back or want picking up.

That has changed. Now if he goes out he will tell us where he is going and also let us know roughly what time he will be back. I also tend to give him a lot more independence, as he is only doing the things he does anyway while he is at the university, and if I didn't let him do it I probably wouldn't see him as often as I do.

Obviously he likes his independence now and doesn't like being my little baby anymore, as he does get quite angry when I do this. When he comes home from the university I always send him back with some food and maybe a little bit of money as well. He doesn't ask for this, but I just feel that he is my baby and I feel as though I am still providing for him, if I at least know he is eating right and has enough money.

are willing to prolong their children's dependency by providing them with the economic means and support to avoid assuming full adult responsibilities for an extended period of time (Kloep & Hendry, 2010). In a sense it has become a relational "game between the generations" (e.g., Scabini, Marta, & Lanz, 2006).

Thus, many young people are given the opportunity to stay longer in education to invest in their own future (which coincides with the economic needs of society) and to delay choices of profession and lifestyle. On the other hand, with the old values becoming dysfunctional and obsolete, the value guidelines that made it easier and quicker for generations before to make these choices are missing. Whereas identity foreclosure—or contented stagnation—may have been functional in a different type of society, the need to make decisions on the basis of reason and experience makes a prolonged moratorium necessary for an increasing number of young people. However, this prolonged period of trying to give meaning to their lives, without guidance from traditions, parents, or older role models, leaves young people vulnerable to aggressive marketing strategies that sell them fashion labels as markers for identity, and advertising logos and slogans as norms to live by (Côté, 2000).

However, in some life domains many young people in highly industrialized societies have made transitions to adulthood far earlier than their peers in agricultural societies—they have much higher discretionary spending power, higher education, earlier sexual initiation, and are far less under the mentorship of adults. On the other hand, they may take far longer to assume adult responsibilities in areas of self-maintenance, economy, and work (Martín, 2002).

BOX 5.2 "I Probably Shouldn't Do Everything for Him"—Mother of an 18-Year-Old Unemployed Son

He's a typical teenage boy; he gets very moody at times and thinks that he knows everything about everything, but he doesn't. He can be quite arrogant and lazy . . . but you know, he's just a typical boy, he needs to be led in the right direction. There is lack of motivation and a lack of concentration; he can't really be bothered to do things; he doesn't want to get out of bed in the morning and when he does get up, all he wants to do is just lounge about in the front room and watch the telly. He should be getting a job, but at the moment he's had a bit of trouble with his knee, so that's another excuse he's got for not getting a job.

I mean, when I was his age it was so different; I had a job and was a lot more independent. Its so different now though; these days, things are different; kids aren't settling down so young anymore. I wouldn't have got away with doing what he does, not working and staying in bed all day.

When he was younger, he was going out with his friends and getting into a bit of trouble here and there, nothing too serious, just the trouble young boys get into. Then I would shout, but it didn't really make

(Continued)

BOX 5.2 (*Cont'd*)

much difference. I didn't shout a lot, not enough, definitely not enough. I didn't really discipline him as such. I was laid back; shouting doesn't work anyway. I was too soft, definitely far too soft. I let him get away with a bit more than I should have done I suppose, and perhaps I should have made sure that when I said "be home on time" that he was home on time. I should have had more rules. If he didn't do something or he did something wrong, I should have disciplined him by taking things away or not letting him out, but I always gave in.

I still look after him, do his washing, ironing, cooking, cleaning, picking up after him sometimes, and just generally doing things that I've always done for him more or less. It's still the same as when he was a child. He thinks he's an adult, but he's not when it comes to going to the hospital, or to the dentist, or something; its "MUM—come with me" so really, me thinking he's growing up, he's still, he's still my baby boy really. He doesn't help out very much. He's 18 years old now though; I think I should get him to help out more. I probably shouldn't do everything for him, like when he was younger; he needs to grow up and I probably shouldn't treat him like a I did when he was a child.

This phenomenon is interlinked with the economic basis of Western societies. Thus, an extremely prolonged moratorium is observable only in highly industrialised countries, and even there mainly in the affluent middle classes, because large sections of the population cannot afford a lengthy education. Societies, which are in the process of industrialisation, or are still predominantly agrarian, have little or no period of moratorium available to young people, whereas in postmodern societies, we will find those who do not want to, and those who cannot, those who choose to, and those who have to, delay their transitions to adulthood. There will be those who grow up very quickly, and those who may never truly grow up to full adult responsibilities.

The Impact of Institutional and Governmental Policies

Young people's developmental pathways are also influenced by institutional and governmental policies in different cultural settings. For example, policies regarding pregnant teenagers have an enormous impact on the further life chances of young women. In Mozambique, Togo, Mali, and Zanzibar, they are expelled from school when it is found they are pregnant and not allowed to return, which means the end of their education. In Kenya, South Africa, and Zambia, pregnant young women must "drop out" of school (though they can be readmitted after a year), which makes further education more difficult, but not impossible. On the other hand, in Namibia, Peru, and Chile, as in most European countries, pregnant teenagers can continue their education, so that one nonnormative shift does not necessarily lead to another (Lloyd et al., 2005).

On a less dramatic note, whether young people have much choice in experimenting with different academic subjects in their education depends on school and university policies. In China, they cannot change subjects once they have started on a university course (Nelson & Chen, 2007), in Spain, length of study is not restricted, allowing for the "eternal student" (Douglass, 2007), whereas in Germany and the UK there are time limits on how long an individual can remain at a university. In England and Wales, but not Scotland where higher education is free for young Scots, study fees are so high that only the wealthy can afford to switch courses often and begin a new study discipline.

As Douglass (2007) has shown for Europe, another factor impinging on developmental pathways is governmental policies on benefits. Youth policies try to standardize transitions as young people fight to find autonomous paths (Machado País, 2002), but the welfare systems of Europe differ in how young people are subsidized in becoming independent. In Scandinavia, young people can receive a governmental loan for their studies, which is not means tested for parental income, and housing benefits are available. This makes it possible for young Swedes to leave their parental home early (the earliest in Europe), and by the age of 25 years most of them have settled into a job and are living independently (Cook & Furstenberg, 2002).

In Mediterranean countries, where state help is weak and unemployment is high, young people have to rely on their families for economic help (Breen & Buchmann, 2002; Rusconi, 2004). Douglass (2005) quotes young Spaniards as being quite happy with the situation, giving them both security and freedom to explore life without the constraints of having to care for a household of their own. It is not uncommon for them to remain in the parental home until their mid-30s. However, Martín (2002) found that only a minority of Spanish youngsters were happy with the situation and would prefer to live independently, if they could. These contradictory findings might stem from the fact that there are different groups in society experiencing a prolonged moratorium: those who can afford to delay independence and choose to do so (as the middle class sample researched by Douglass, 2005) and those who are prevented from being independent because of unemployment and high housing costs (who were part of the statistics used by Martín, 2002).

In Germany, child support is given to parents, so that it is often more economical for young people to stay at home during their education (Breen & Buchman, 2002; Douglass, 2007). Due to the apprenticeship system, youth unemployment is not as high as in other countries, though employment opportunities are scarce, so that young people tend to retain jobs rather than experiment with various careers. They even reconstruct their self-biographies to convince themselves that a training place they accepted simply because it was the only one available, was what they always actually wanted (Heinz, 1987).

In the liberal economy of Britain, minimal welfare is available, study fees and housing costs are high, and youth unemployment is relatively high (Breen & Buchmann, 2002). Thus, two types of young people emerge who seemingly superficially fit the description of emergent adults: living in the parental home and delaying career decisions, thoughts of marriage, and children (Hendry & Kloep, 2010). One group consists of the typical students from the more affluent middle classes as Arnett and Tanner describe them, taking their time to explore their identities and delaying adult responsibilities. The other group, however, does not deliberately postpone entry into the adult world: these people are prevented from doing so by their lack resources. Often, their educational level is low, so they are not able to find steady employment. Without an income, there is no way they can move out of the parental home, because their parents do not have the means to support independent living; and for the same reason they cannot afford to start a family.

BOX 5.3   "Cos I'm Not Good at It, See"—16-Year-Old Unemployed Male

I don't go to school no more, they call me—I think it's a disaffected male youth. So that's what I am! All I do really is watch TV and bum around. Life is so boring. I hated school cos I don't get stuff, and the teachers were always putting me down; then the kids start to rip it out of me, and that makes me angry, which means I fight. I don't get into trouble on purpose, I've told them all this, but they don't take notice. Every one says I'm crap, so that's what I am, no surprises there.

My ideal day would be where I hang around with people who make me feel good, 'cos everybody thinks they know me, but do they hell! I don't even know me, so there's bound to be summat good in me somewhere . . . I'm afraid I will be stuck like this for good—that's scary, but it's probably what's gonna happen unless someone shows me what to do, but who en it? I just wanna have summat I'm good at like . . . I sit around and if I'm honest, I don't even watch the tele. 'cos I think a lot, about me and how c**p things are. I think they're gonna try me on one of these alternative education program things—it won't be much use though 'cos I'm not good at it, see.

"If I Could Find Something I'm Good at . . ."—18-Year-Old Young Offender

Why would anybody want to know me, really? I haven't got a lot going for me and no real ideas about what to do. I finished school with nothing really nearly 2 years now. I haven't got a Mum and Dad, but Nan and Granch do all they can to get me about, but it's a bit hard for them 'cos they're old.

I got to learn to chill out, but I expect to get stuff wrong, and got no faith in what I'm like. I reckon 'cos if I let people know me I might not like what they see, 'cos not many would stick around with me. If I could find something I'm good at, that's not gonna happen though, 'cos I'm too s**t scared of stuff. If I could ever find a talent, then I could feel a bit better about myself.

'Cos a kid with a track record like mine don't get nobody interested in. I've see it on the tele, where people like me end up living on their own, in s**tty run down flats . . . I know what I am and I don't need no tele to tell me, but I can't change it but no matter what. I'd like to tell other kids not to do the stuff that I done, 'cos it messes up so much and you cannot just turn the clock back. If I could, I wouldn't have been so lost . . . I mean I don't go nowhere now. Come to think about it, the only time I'm comfortable is when I'm asleep, and I'm not even sure I am then.

Some teenage girls try to resolve this problem of impeded adulthood by getting pregnant, as this entitles them as a single parent to state and housing benefits—perhaps one reason why Britain has the highest rate of teenage pregnancies in Europe (Coleman & Schofield, 2007). In other words, the economic changes in society that lead to widened opportunities for some privileged young people have also widened the gap between them and disadvantaged youth, who, in fact, have less choices now than they had before, as Bynner (2005) has shown.

The Widening Gap

The phenomenon of a widening gap does not exist in Britain alone, nor just in Europe. It is a worldwide trend. In fact, it is Americans who have experienced the greatest increase in income inequality among rich nations over the past decades (Smeeding, 2005). Additionally, the employment structure of many developing economies has changed and continues to change, so that there are fewer jobs in the public sector, leading to increased job insecurity (Quisumbing & Hallman, 2005). In China, the new economic opportunities that contributed to poverty reduction also compete with education, as there are higher costs for schooling now, and the number of unskilled temporary labor migrants is on the increase, adding to the already existing gap between wealthy and poor families (Hannum & Jihong, 2005). Similar disparities are reported from Latin America (Galambos & Martínez, 2007).

Furthermore, in times of individualization, young people have to rely more on family support than on help from the community, which makes those without a family with means particularly vulnerable. Public support is often cut off once young people turn 18 years of age, and many lose access to special education, health care, housing, and protective services, which is particularly difficult for young people with special needs and disabilities (Osgood et al., 2005). Overall, the number of children and adolescents living as refugees, who participate in armed conflict, who are homeless, or who leave school before the legal leaving age has increased dramatically in the past few decades, particularly for children in low-income countries or in low-income communities within countries (Weisner & Lowe, 2005).

In the United States, it is race differences that account for much of the inequalities among young people, with a strikingly high percentage of less-educated African Americans and Puerto Ricans experiencing unemployment, incarceration, homelessness, poverty, and childbearing even before they reach 20 years of age, leading Cook and Furstenberg (2002) to assume that the United States probably has more variation than any other country in the quality of its citizens' transitions to adulthood.

Obviously, structural variables such as gender, class, and race combine with different countries' welfare systems and institutional policies as well as with prevailing value and belief systems to create an enormous heterogeneity in the transitions to adulthood. Reitzle (2006) concluded that "There is obviously no uniform phenomenon of emerging adulthood seizing entire cohorts of young people, not across countries with vastly differing living conditions for young people, and not even within a country" (Reitzle, 2006, p. 35).

However, these influences do not come from wider society alone. They are closely interrelated with processes happening in the immediate microsystems, as we now illustrate in the following section.

Value Systems and Emerging Adulthood

To complicate matters further, the hegemonic, dominant value system that once was instrumental in delaying or preventing societal change is now somewhat dysfunctional in most highly industrialized societies. Though across many years overarching societal values have been endorsed by the majority of the population, they now have only one function: creating security by releasing individuals from making their own decisions—a task that the behavioral guidelines of social norms have always had.

Although no longer being supported by governments via laws (though often propagated by parliamentarians in the media), the old system of family values still survives in some segments of Western culture. Some people defend it for religious reasons and some because education, the new route to success, is not available to them. As a consequence, for some young people transitions to adulthood have changed, whereas others still follow more traditional routes into society. Du-Bois Reymond (1998) demonstrated that young people attempt to direct the content and complexity of their lives, while at the same time adapting to the constantly changing demands of their environment (especially the job market). She identified both "trendsetters," whose life concepts involve "choice biographies" in a way similar to Arnett's emerging adults, and those who are oriented toward a "normal biography" concerning areas of living such as job training and balancing work and living, and influenced by gender and socioeconomic circumstances; this "gap" is widening (e.g., Bynner, 2005, 2008).

The influence of traditions and value systems becomes apparent in the differences between Western industrialized countries and almost all of the rest of the world. In most societies, assuming adult responsibilities takes on a different meaning than in highly individualized cultures: it does not imply taking responsibility for yourself, but rather taking responsibility for the family (Papastefanou, 1999). For example, in Argentina, where significantly more young people than in the United States regard young adulthood as a time for responsibility and commitment to others, family obligations are considered more important than career plans (Facio et al., 2007). Furthermore, this value difference is shown in the fact that young people traditionally stay at home until they marry, and some even after marriage (Arias & Hernández, 2007;

Scabini, Marta, & Lanz, 2006; Galambos & Martínez, 2007; Douglass, 2007; Lanz & Tagliabue, 2007). Characteristically, for emerging adults in Turkey one of their greatest concerns in relation to becoming adults is how to meet the expectations of the extended family when treating them to elaborately prepared meals, and how to maintain contact with relatives living at a distance (Atak & Çok, 2007)—concerns, that to our knowledge, have never been mentioned by Western youth.

Strong family commitments and a feeling of responsibility toward parents—not independence from parents—also prevail among young people in China. An overwhelming majority (89%) consider that being capable of supporting their parents financially is "necessary for adulthood" (Nelson, Badger, & Wu, 2004). The Confucian collective values are so strong that the Chinese Government suspects that they prevent the development of competitive skills. Their new economic strategy has included the training of individualistic values in the school curriculum (Nelson & Chen, 2007). Nevertheless, more than double as many young Chinese as US-Americans in the age range of 18–21 years regard themselves as adults (Badger, Nelson, & Barry, 2006).

The interdependency of the economy, the dominant cultural value system, and education in influencing transitions to adulthood has been effectively demonstrated in a study by Fuligni (2007). He followed Latin American and Asian immigrants over 15 years. Similar to their peers in their countries of origin, young immigrants showed consistently higher ratings on scales measuring family obligation than their white US-American counterparts. This was also true for second-generation immigrants. Living in a country with a different value system had less effect than their country-of-origin's beliefs. However, after some years, one subgroup of Chinese origin slowly changed their value system and became indistinguishable from their white US-American peers. Coming from more affluent families than the other immigrants they could afford a higher education, and once gaining a university degree realized the individualistic career opportunities that lay ahead. This did create a conflict between their own ambitions and family values and caused them to question these values. Thus, merely being surrounded by a different value culture does not have a powerful effect; however, when they engage with the new culture's roles and rules, they start to absorb its values and become part of it.

Another sphere in which values modify pathways to adulthood is the different opportunities for social experiences and exploration offered on the basis of gender. Machismo in Latin America, for example, restricts freedom for young women even in the more affluent classes (Galambos & Martínez, 2007). Indian girls often do not have the freedom to choose whom and when to marry (Mitchell, 2004), whereas even in present-day Japan, a woman without children is not regarded as an adult, and an unmarried woman is still registered as the daughter of her father and not in her own right. The transition to adulthood is not complete unless she marries and has children (Rosenberger, 2007). And even though the gap between male and female school enrollment is closing worldwide, there are still many countries in which girls are denied an education (in Pakistan, 15% of men but 46% of women lack formal schooling; Lloyd & Grant, 2007; and in Cameroon, where only one member of a family can afford to attend school, an increasing number of girls leave school early because they cannot pay the fees; Kuate-Defo, 2005). In Western and Middle Africa, the percentage of young women giving birth before 18 years of age remains in excess of 30% (Lloyd, 2005), and is extremely high among the poor in rural regions of Latin America (Galambos & Martínez, 2007). In all these examples a period of extended moratorium is denied young women on the basis of old patriarchal values and beliefs.

Microsystems

Macrosystemic changes on a societal level are reflected in cultural microsystems. We have outlined above how transformations from an agrarian to a postmodern society change the statuses and roles of the young. From being seen and treated as an economic investment, many young people are now seen as an expensive emotional asset. Some couples are prepared to make many sacrifices, both economically and medically, to be able to have children. This, in turn, has an effect on parenting styles. Corporal punishment is now forbidden by law in many European countries, and authoritarian parenting is on the decline. In a study of 10,000 young people in the UK (Hendry et al., 1993; Shucksmith et al., 1995) the most commonly perceived parenting style was *"permissive parenting."* Parents often give in to the "pester-power" of their children at a young age (John & Alwyn, 2005), so that it is not necessary for teenagers to fight for their freedom, having already won this battle long before! Consequently, teenagers do not consider "conflicts with their parents" as a particular concern (Kloep, 1999; Settersten et al., 2005).

Scabini et al. (2006) describe the changing relationship between teenagers and their parents in Italy as follows:

> The path young Italians take towards the achievement of autonomy
> from their families is not characterized by a series of trials and attempts
> at distancing themselves from the parental home until the right
> moment to leave arrives, once and for all. Rather, it is a slow and

progressive restructuring of the relationship with parents based on a belief in the necessity of prolonging cohabitation due to objective, external difficulties (the difficulty of finding a first job or of keeping a job) as well as on the reciprocal psychological advantage for all concerned. (Scabini et al., 2006, p. 23)

Indeed, according to Scabini et al. (2006) the slowing down of the transition to adulthood is possible only because young adults can count on their families.

The transmission of values within the family context is an important element in young adults' development (Barry, Padilla-Walker, Madsen, & Nelson, 2008; Knafo & Schwartz, 2009; Roest, Dubas, & Gerris, 2009; Zentner & Renaud, 2007). Nevertheless, in some cases, the emotional bond to children can lead to overindulgence and overprotection. The continuance of familial support for the separation–individuation processes during adolescence and early adulthood demonstrates how family relationships, and perceived attachments, fluctuate and change as the parent and adult child generations separately, and conjointly, progress along their life courses (e.g., Kloep & Hendry, 2010; Scabini & Marta, 2006). Seiffge-Krenke (2007) has shown that *overprotective* parenting leads to overdependence and reduced autonomy in early adulthood, whereas Côté (2000) claimed that when parents do not give guidance and structure (important for identity formation) or offer few values and beliefs for young people to rebel against, a context for delaying adulthood is created. Côté's conclusion is that a significant number of young adults now have difficulties in managing their lives, and the greatest problems come to those with least economic, intellectual, and psychological resources.

Apart from not being very effective in educating their children to take responsibilities, some parents do not encourage independence, and actively strive to keep their children at home. They willingly provide them with services and material support, do not burden them with domestic chores, and do not make financial demands on them (Douglass, 2005), so that young people do not have many incentives to begin an independent life, but associate adulthood with onerous responsibility (Thomson, & Holland, 2002).

In our interviews with 56 parents of emerging adults in Wales (Kloep & Hendry, 2010), a few parents complained about the lack of autonomy in their children, although some indicated that they actually provided the "perfect" environment for their offspring's contented stagnation, mainly because they did not want to let their children go.

This parental attitude appears to be an adaptation to the ongoing socioeconomic changes in Western societies. Only 20 years ago, parents were less

BOX 5.4 "I Have to Now Find a Place in Her Life"—Mother of a 19-Year-Old Daughter

She has shown great independence, particularly over the past 18 months. She has managed to start to build up a business and she has been able to do that reasonably successfully, without too much advice and help from me. She has researched things independently and has gone out of her way to try to improve her knowledge with regards to the type of business she has as a working woman. She is definitely an adult; she is a working woman, and she has got a long-term relationship with a chap.

I think that in some ways I felt closer to her a few years ago, because the fact that she has grown in independence and doesn't need me in the same way sometimes makes me feel like I am on the side line. But I do feel this is a natural part of growing up and actually that is what should be happening. I think that made me feel vulnerable, because I have to now find my place in her life. There will be a place somewhere . . . I know there will but it's just a case of me finding it and from me moving from being mum and relied on to being mum of an independent young woman who is branching out and going into the big wide world.

enthusiastic about their offspring delaying departure from the family home. They regarded the "incomplete launch" of their adult children as a failure of their parenting skills and a disappointment of their parental expectations (Schnaiberg & Goldenberg, 1989). Now, this nonnormative procedure of living with grown-up children has become a quasinormative event, and parents seem to embrace their role as near-eternal care-givers. For instance, parents in Britain have over the past few years started to accompany their children not only to "open days" and admission interviews at universities, but also to job interviews and wage negotiations. This overprotection by parents is paralleled by similar tendencies of overprotection in schools and other youth organizations (e.g., Caldwell, 2007; Kloep & Hendry, 2007). With regard to education, Levine (2005; Levine & Wagner 2005a, 2005b) has written that many young people in their mid-20s lack self-awareness, do not have organizational, decision-making skills, lack communication and alliance-building abilities, and do not possess the insights and qualities that are necessary for the transitions into working life. He believes that education leaves young people unready to move into adulthood because they are overindulged, and uncommitted to deep, focused and detailed learning. In treating young persons as immature and in need of protection, parents and teachers may slow down the process of maturation.

Resources and Challenges in Daily Life

Having discussed adolescent transformations on a macrosystemic and a microsystemic level, we now turn to individual experiences and proactivity in the process of growing up. Even in the Western industrialized world, just over 50% of the young people in most countries are in higher education (Coleman & Brooks, 2009) and can experience emerging adulthood in the way that Arnett and Tanner describe. Bynner (2005) and Côté and Bynner (2008) have proposed a growing "gap" between the social classes in both the UK and Canada in terms of psychosocial resources, possibilities, and opportunities. Thus, it is possible to suggest a number of broad subgroups (with many individual differences) of transitional pathways from adolescence to adulthood. We have already described (Hendry & Kloep, 2010) from our qualitative study in Wales that there exists, apart from typical emerging adults, a group of young people that does not take on adult responsibilities for a prolonged period of time, simply because they do not possess the necessary resources and skills to enter the adult world of work and independent living, and are thus denied the opportunity to do so. In addition, we also discovered a third group: those who already felt and behaved "like an adult" in their late teenage years.

BOX 5.5 "I Have the Right to Call Myself an Adult"—18-Year-Old Female

I've got four children to look after as a live-in nanny. I started off as a nursery nurse and decided to become a nanny. It's always been a dream. I've always loved children and I always hoped that I would be good with children. I probably felt like that from about age 11 years, wanting to work with children. In a normal day I get up about 7, get the kids up at half past 7. First I get the older ones up and dressed and then I go and get the baby dressed, give her a bottle, take all the children to school at 9, and then go back and look after just the baby in the morning.

She has a bottle, then she sleeps about an hour or so, and then I get all the housework done. I go off, pick B up from nursery at 12, then spend the afternoon painting and doing something creative with them or take them to the park. In the afternoon I go and pick C up from school at half past 3, then I go back home. I usually do something with both the boys, either cooking or something like that, maybe bake a cake; I then cook tea about half past 5, get them all bathed and everything by about half past 6, and get then in bed by 7. All of them.

If I ever did change my career, it would be something that was in childcare. I'd like to have children of my own while I am still young, so obviously not too old. I'd like to get married between 25 and 30 years and then become a childminder, I think. I hope I will find someone in the next 2 years hopefully. It's just a matter of meeting someone.

I consider myself as a young adult. Well I'm old enough to bring up four children, day in and day out, and I have to take on all the responsibilities of an adult, so I think I have the right to call myself an adult.

I don't get to see my family and friends very often. I live with my employer and I rent a room as a live-in nanny. My family would see me as an adult I think. I think its not about age, it's about taking on responsibilities. I have made my decisions for life; things may change later on, but everything in my mind is set out about what I want and how I'm going to get it, and I can't see that ever changing. I'll do anything for the life I've already planned, but if I meet someone who I really love and they don't want children, then I don't know how I will end up coping with that. Obviously I want my own house, but I might not be able to afford it. Childcare is not good money.

I've based all my decisions on my own and done what I want. It was hard, because my mum wanted me to go to college, and I said no, I wanted to take a gap year and do what I wanted to do, and I did. She said I would never get into a career after having a gap year, but I've proved her wrong and then I went into doing an apprenticeship. She still said "go to college," but I was having none of it. I know what I want. I've made all my own decisions. I'd rather do something that I enjoy and not regret what I've done in later life. It was important that I did what I felt was right. That's why I did the gap year. I tried everything. I had 15 different jobs. I tried every single type of job going and I realized that I hated them all, so now I'm happy just to stick with childcare, because I've got everything out of my system and I'm doing things the way I want. I tried to be a cleaner, shop assistant, chip shop, I was an assistant manager, I was a waitress, a chef in a pizza place, I worked behind a bar, I worked in the cricket ground taking money for the tickets, I don't know, I tried a bit of everything really; I did street marketing and things like that. Then I did

(Continued)

BOX 5.5   *(Cont'd)*

some volunteer work. . ... Everything. I enjoyed it, but I didn't get the same satisfaction out of that than I get out of childcare. Apart from the money, you don't get anything else back.

"I'm Rather Mature for My Age"—20-Year-Old Married Man

In fact, it is my first regular job, save for some part-time gigs I did when I was younger. I am security tech at the factory warehouse. I watch the monitors and sometimes walk the perimeter and check to see that no one tries to steal our junk. It's well paid, given that I dropped out of college and don't have a good education, and it is quite easy. It's a bit boring and I usually have no one to talk to, so I usually read books if I have one around. Well, I like that security stuff, and that's a professional experience, isn't it? Maybe later I'll be able to get into one of the security companies and work for some corp or something like that. I'd love to. I have some friends who are working in banks and other high-profile places and they say it's really good. My supervisor is pleased with my work, and as the warehouses are part of the company infrastructure, maybe I'll have the chance to work at main facilities. You know—a high-profile place means better money, better experience, and better opportunities. And then, who knows.

People say I'm rather mature for my age. Especially now being married and all. I had some girlfriends before, but, in fact, I started late. I was 14 or 15 years old when I was with my first. Then there were several more, you know; I couldn't be with one more than several months, but that's normal, isn't it. But then I met M and bang! I was in real love at first sight, man! I talked to my mother and then to her parents; for several months we were together and then we got married. We understand each other; I love her, she loves me. I think it is the first person I trust so much. We share many interests, maybe that's why. She's 3 years older, is graduating this year, and friends say she is more serious than me.

It was her idea to marry so quickly. And I agreed. I imagine we'll be happy together. That's how I see it now. I hope it won't change. I think I got more serious, too. You know, now we're planning our next moves. That is moving to our own flat, how to handle money—things like that. I never planned like that before.

Well, I still feel young, very young. I've got a job and I am married. But I still don't have my own house, and I have the same friends and interests I had before. So it wasn't any great change for me. Maybe . . . (pause) I don't know. Maybe I was an adult long before I turned 18. Before that I used to hang out for no purpose, but now I do it only when I want a good time. And when I have time, that is. Adulthood means being mature, responsible, really independent, as well as financially independent. But I started to look for a job quite early. I tried to live on my own; now I am married and feel good about it, so there wasn't any great change. But, you know, we live still with our parents and we move to our own flat in a month or two. Maybe that will change something. I think there is no such thing as a border between adulthood and youth, you know. Some people think it is when you hit 18, right? Or when you have sex. But that's c**p. Some say it's when you get a job and start to live by yourself and that makes more sense. I know some of my friends for several years and now they have jobs and families; some have kids, but they haven't changed much. When you say "adult" I imagine my parents and other people that are, say, 40 now, but well . . . they seem boring. And many people I know never gave up the fun, they're the same people they were.

What was it that made them "grow up" earlier than their peers? They all reported a range of life events that had made them take on responsibility for themselves, and for others, from an early age. Some had to care for disabled parents or had to support a parent after bereavement or divorce, and some had to look after younger siblings or had a child of their own. Some felt financially independent because their parents had no resources to support them (e.g., Evans, 2007). All agreed that having found a job had made them more mature than their peers who were still within the educational system, because they had more responsibilities, and interacted with older colleagues who treated them as equals. They saw their time at school as a "meaningless" period with few interests or demands; in fact, they had "voted with their feet" and not attended school much during their last year within the educational system.

In this manner, their maturity had been achieved because they developed personally through "steeling experiences" (Rutter, 1996) and learned resilience through nonnormative shifts. Internal markers of adulthood (e.g., taking responsibility for your actions, making independent decisions, becoming financially independent, establishing equal relations with parents) appear to be of greater salience than external markers (e.g., marriage, parenthood, beginning full-time work) for their personal self-classification of being "adult" (e.g., Arnett, 2003, 2004; Barry & Nelson, 2005). "Growing up early" adds to young people's psychosocial resources and their views of adult status. Hence, there are many developmental tasks other than marriage, employment, and leaving home that can contribute to transformation and development. The achievement of tasks and the successful meeting of challenges to gain "steel-ing" experiences are the gateways to becoming adult; the so-called "markers" are merely "signposts on the road," and these can be inconsistent and varied in a changing society. By coping with tasks—not by simply getting older!—skills are learned that allow young people to meet responsibilities with the nec-essary experience to handle them. In similar vein, Westberg (2004) has commented on how those who felt they had made the transition to adulthood believed that the *processes* gone through were the most significant elements of achievement and assisted the young person's transformation toward adult-hood. This is further supported by the findings of a longitudinal qualitative study by Henderson et al. (2007), who concluded that

> it is through the experience of competence in particular areas of their lives, that young people come to make investments of time and energy that have significance for their trajectories . . . The investments in different areas play an important part in the construction of identity and adulthood. (Henderson et al., 2007, p. 58)

These findings provide vivid illustrations of our resource-challenge model. It is the normative and nonnormative shifts that the individual encounters that create opportunities for development. If young people are faced with adult-like responsibilities, they will become adults in the process. If they are "wrapped in cotton-wool" and protected from challenges, they will not. If the challenges outweigh the young person's resources then their further development might be put at risk. Adult maturity is earned, and is not a matter of years!

Concluding Comments

In summary, the experience of emerging adulthood seems to be dependent on whether a prolonged moratorium is the result of cultural and economic forces, of policies, prevailing values, parental styles, and nonnormative shifts, which give the individual either choice or constraints; and whether the period is used effectively: during this moratorium some may acquire skills for adult living and others may idle their time away (see Fig. 5.1).

Furthermore, what we hope to have demonstrated in this chapter are the powers of a systemic multilevel theoretical framework to provide tools to

BOX 5.6 "It's All Just Made Me Lose Interest in Me"—17-Year-Old Female
Young Carer

I am 17 years old and I am a young carer. I do find it difficult because
I can't go out and do things normal teenagers do. Not only because I look
after both my parents, but also cos I'm afraid to leave them. If summat
was to happen to them, I would never forgive myself. I get up every day
at 7 in the morning and wake up my younger sister and get her ready for
school, cos she can be a bit lazy in the morning. But she should be able
to have things as normal as possible, and cos I never did it, it makes me
wanna do it for her all the more.

Then I get all the tablets and medications sorted, and then work
about the house. Because they both suffer with serious mental illness,
I have to make sure that they feel comfortable and happy all the time,
because they might get upset and then it gets hard. . ..

I'm glad I don't have to go to school no more, cos I was really bullied
there. Sometimes I feel like I'm missing out cos I could never have a
boyfriend, they would go mad, and anyway, I don't get time to make
myself look good, cos I'm always cleaning, cooking, sorting meds, talking
to doctors and social workers, and stuff.

I would like to be a nursery nurse, but mam and dad have to be my
priority. When I was younger I had all these great ideas about being a
teacher . . . It's all just made me lose interest in me. I don't know what
I would do if I wasn't a carer, cos—that's me now, it's who I am. I think
caring for my parents is what I'll always do, even though I think I could
do more. . ..

"I'm Scared of Having to Do This Forever"—18-Year-Old Male Young Carer

I am 18 years old. I care for my brother and my mother; they both have
depression and are mentally ill. Dad left, he couldn't cope. I cook, clean,
wash, drive, shop, and feed and clothe my family on a daily basis; it's hard
going, but I'm ok. I just wish I could get a bit more help. Social services
don't really help that much, and don't seem to take me seriously. So my
days are basically always the same. It's been ages since I did what
I enjoyed—years!

I would like to have some time to experiment and find me. But it's
not going to happen, and I'd feel too guilty. I love my family, but I'm

(Continued)

BOX 5.6 *(Cont'd)*

scared of having to do this forever. I am afraid I will have to do this for good; there's worse things, we could all be dead. I don't do anything for me really, and I'd say I am a shy person. The problem is, no one wants to hear the truth, because it doesn't look good for them. If just my mother and my brother became well, I could have a really normal life then. I've always wondered what it would be like, but I find it very hard to imagine. Routine is all that keeps me going at the moment, cos I sit down sometimes and I'm drained, fed up, and in need of a rest.

interpret and understand the processes involved in life span transitions and transformations. This is because the fairly rapid changes in societies worldwide in destandardizing the life course mean it is no longer possible to analyze, in traditional terms of stages and states, how economic shifts (and globalization) create new pathways and roles in development for different groups of young people.

What we have done is to take young peoples' transitions toward adulthood as an example of the interactive mechanisms of transformation. It would be equally possible to reveal the important factors of this process at any point in the life course: transitions to middle age, emerging old age, the heterogeneity

BOX 5.7 "I've Had to Grow up a Lot Quicker"—20-Year-Old Mother

I am an adult, because I have got a 2-year-old child, so I've had to grow up a lot quicker than most teenagers did, because I had a child to look after. When I'm working, I get up, I have breakfast, see to my daughter, who is 2, get her dressed and what have you, change myself, and then I get on the bus and go to work. Then my mother has my daughter. Then I come home, obviously I'm here with her then, and then we'll have food and then we'll play about with whatever she decides she wants to do.

If I've got to go out somewhere, down the shops, she'll come with me; that is about it, really. I've got responsibilities now, obviously, because I've got a daughter to look after, so it's not just me I've got to think about now. I obviously work as well, part time, so I've got to arrange things for work and things like that, so just that responsibility really about being a parent. It's not too bad for me, because I still live with my parents, so my mother is usually at hand. I have got friends and family that will help and I've got a younger sister that will help as well, if I need her to. If I decide to go out, which isn't very often now, but if there is a special occasion with my friends where it's her birthday or something, and it's a Friday or Saturday night, I will ask my mum to baby-sit for that occasion.

I was doing my A levels[1] when I got pregnant when I was 17, so I was in second year A levels. I was pregnant and than I had her in December and then I went back to finish my A levels off. I chose not to go to the university because of my daughter. I was working part-time in a shop anyway, so that's what I just carried on doing. I like working in a shop, I enjoy it, and it's a couple of hours out of the house. It's a way of meeting new people, so hopefully I'll meet my new man in my shop. I'm a shop assistant; I have worked in a shop since I was old enough to work, since I was 16; I always worked doing my GCSEs. I would like to work with children perhaps. I always said when I was in school that I'd like to be a teacher, but obviously I became pregnant and it didn't work out. Perhaps I would like to go in and be a teacher's helper, that is something I'd look for when she is older and when she is in school. My daughter—everything is based around her, it's just her and my job obviously, because I need that to have money to well support her. It's my mother really that I depend on, because she baby-sits a lot for me. Obviously I'm living with my parents so eventually we would look to move out, but not yet; that could be a few years down the line. If I meet someone then we'll probably set up a home, which would be a nice thing to look forward to.

---

1 Higher level exam in a number of chosen subjects at British secondary schools that enables the pupil to apply for university.

of pathways into retirement—they all possess the same mechanisms, the same dynamics within the processes of economic change, and the accompanying transformations in the value systems on the macrolevel and microlevel.

Here, we have discussed how recent economic forces have created new pathways in young peoples' transitions—and under what conditions these have created a new age stage for a growing number of young people in varying societies. In this chapter, systemic analysis has additionally shown that these economic–cultural shifts present other pathways for those who cannot, or do not want to, respond "appropriately" to these demands, and particular "fast route" transitions for those who respond to nonnormative forces by rapidly developing mature skills through "steeling" experiences.

If we extend our analysis into the future, we could speculate about forth-coming changes and what they might look like. The need for unskilled work will decrease even further in the richest countries, because they will acquire cheap labor in poorer countries. Increasingly, this is equally true for those with a university education. For the richer nations this will mean a growing number of individuals following various patterns of extended moratorium be it imposed or self-chosen; however, for many in the poorer countries, it will initiate "early adulthood."

In addition, the ongoing high technology revolution might change the role of young people significantly. In general, they are more "in tune" with new information technology (IT) developments than adults, a fact that could allow the technologically skillful to gain highly paid jobs at a younger and younger age. This would enable them to become economically independent of their parents and take on adult responsibilities, thus shortening their transitions to adulthood, at least in some life domains. Increasing affluence and the pos-sibility to work from home—or from anywhere in the world—might also influ-ence their social life and health behaviors. In other words, we might have to identify yet another form of lifestyle for a minority—and recognize the possible heterogeneity of life transitions within new societal change.

Given the potential strength of systemic analysis in explaining human change on the microlevel and macrolevel of any society at any historical time, compared to the patchwork "plastering" of inventing new stages each time society changes, and having to adapt them to explain a million different indi-vidual circumstances, we conclude this chapter by stating that a theory describ-ing "many different emerging adulthoods" as a normative stage in human development is not a particularly powerful instrument for understanding human change. In fact, no stage theory is—let's remove them!

SECTION III

Rejoinders

6

Rejoinder to Chapters 2 and 3: Critical Comments on Arnett's and Tanner's Approach

Marion Kloep and Leo B. Hendry

Why the Concept Is Not a Theory

As we have argued, and as Arnett has admitted, the concept of emerging adulthood is not relevant for many young people in parts of the Third World. Given that the overwhelming majority of young people today live in these countries, this reduces the significance of his "theory" to roughly 14% of the world's youth population (Lloyd et al., 2005). Furthermore, Arnett (2007a) admits that the luxury of an extended moratorium is restricted to the affluent middle classes, and does not exist in the poorer areas of Europe, nor for many young immigrant, ethnic minorities, nor for those who have little education or a disability. So simply presenting a concept, which selectively focuses on those young people who do have a lengthy early adulthood without having to assume adult roles and responsibilities, reduces the numbers for whom his new framework is valid, both selectively and significantly.

We already know that many of those with a prolonged moratorium are forced to remain within their parents' household, because they have access neither to a university education nor to a well-paid job. They are neither happy nor optimistic regarding their future (Hendry & Kloep, 2007a, 2010) and can thus not be considered as archetypes of Arnett's emerging adults. Nor would

Arnett want to include those who have married young and care for families of their own, or the talented young professionals in the areas of sports, performing arts, information technology (IT), modeling, international investing, and the armed forces, to name but a few, who have committed early to a career. For example, professional cricketers have their career behind them and face retirement in their late 20s, whereas some of their age peers still have not decided on a permanent job (Roberts, 2009) (Box 6.1).

BOX 6.1   "It's Too Late Now and Too Much Money Has Been Spent"—18-Year-Old Professional Golfer

I'm not really doing anything at the moment except playing golf. I did go to college for a year to do A-levels, but have now decided to pursue golf as a career. I play everyday, except for Thursdays, which is when I have a day off. I'm hoping to start a PGA golf course next March, so that I can become a golf teacher.

I still live at home with my parents and my younger sister. I'm really looking forward to moving out, so that I can be independent, but I will miss my family though, we are very close. I have to move away because there are better opportunities outside Wales. I am looking forward to having my own place; I'm 18 years old now, but my mum still treats me like a baby half the time! I'm looking forward to going out clubbing; my parents don't like me going out clubbing too much 'cause they worry and nag me about what time I'll be in and all that. I'll also be paid while I train; I think it's about £200 per week.

I don't really do anything at home; everything gets done for me, you know, washing my clothes, etc., and doing my food; I think I'll be in for a shock when I move away, but my mum has said that she'll come and get my washing for me!

I don't want to share with anyone, I want to have my own place, so I am hoping that daddy will buy me a flat. He would love me to have a good job to do with golf, so I think he will do that for me; they can afford it!

I've been playing golf since I was about 4 or 5 years old so I can't do anything else to be honest. My dad also plays golf, but not to the standard I play; he didn't really have the support I had when he was younger, so I want to do it for him as well. If I did really well, they, my dad in particular, would be so proud of me.

I was quite good in school though; I'm quite hardworking. I left school with 10 GCSEs[1], so I suppose I could have done something else; I don't know, it's too late now and too much money has been spent anyway.

Sometimes I feel pressured to do well, 'cause I'd like to do well so that they haven't wasted their money; I wouldn't want to let them down. Sometimes though I feel as if I've missed out on friends and stuff like that, 'cause on a Saturday I was always playing golf with my dad and sometimes I didn't really want to, but I wouldn't have said that to him.

My girlfriend of a year is a bit bossy and sometimes she thinks I spend too much time playing golf and that I should spend more time with her, like on the weekends and stuff, and she doesn't really like me going out clubbing with my friends; she gets jealous! She does get on my nerves sometimes. Most of the time we are happy, but we do have arguments now and then, mostly about golf and my friends; she thinks she runs my life. We will move in together when I go away; hopefully it will be good. She does not really like golf, but from my point of view she will just have to accept it, because that's what I'll be doing.

---

[1] General Certificate of Secondary Education: This is the basic subject examination that a majority of British teenagers aspire to. It does not qualify the young person to attend university.

Thus, when Arnett (2007a) states that "most young Europeans enjoy the benefit of this general affluence and experience a long and leisurely emerging adulthood," he refers mainly (or exclusively?) to those in higher education. This leaves us with a very restricted group of young people that can be subdivided further into those who use their period of extended moratorium to widen their horizons by traveling, working in voluntary services overseas, and exploring opportunities in work and education, and those who spend their time partying and living a hedonistic and often parasitic life. In sum, we can use Arnett's own words, published in a different context, to comment on his "theory": "The result is an understanding of psychology that it is incomplete and does not adequately represent humanity" (Arnett, 2008, p. 602)."

In other words, emerging adulthood is not a developmental stage, it is a particular range of lifestyles. Those who choose Arnett's "emerging adult" lifestyle may actually have less in common with many of their age peers, and more in common with wealthy, fun-loving, hedonistic teenagers or even with affluent people in retirement, who spend their time exploring new job opportunities, traveling widely, developing new hobbies, finding new romantic partners and socializing with friends, thereby spending the much-hoped for inheritance of their emergent adult-children on a long and leisurely emerging old age!

The mere description of a new lifestyle, limited to a certain age-cohort in certain societies at a certain historical time within particular socioeconomic conditions, cannot be regarded as a theory: it neither adds explanation nor prediction. It is even restricted in its descriptive powers because of its limited generalizability. Furthermore, it will almost certainly become outdated, since Western societies are bound to change and new cohorts emerge with different developmental characteristics in different social contexts. For comparison, just imagine the scientific value a medical theory would have if it limited its explanations of human digestion based solely on people who eat pastas! The natural sciences would never accept a theory whose laws change from place to place. The law of gravity, for example, applies equally well in Wales or Massachusetts or even on the moon—and that is because environmental differences between the places have already been integrated into the law (Greene, 2004). Why should the social sciences be satisfied with less? Thus, Arnett's approach belongs to the kind of developmental frameworks that are now regarded as anachronistic:

> A decade ago, developmental psychology could easily be characterized as a field in search of ontological unity, marked by increasingly particularistic, domain- and context-specific "mini-theories," which offered a narrow focus on specific behaviours in specific settings, but at the price of an integrated developmental account. (Witherington, 2007, p. 127)

Such trends, if not paradigm shifts, occur across many disciplines. For example, even Darwin's doctrines about the evolution of species have been improved on by looking at organisms as developing and transforming dynamic systems to explain the structure and change in organisms (Webster & Goodwin, 1996).

Why the Concept Is Not New

Historically, there have always been privileged groups in society who could afford lengthy voyages of self-discovery: studying and learning, seeking their identity, and exploring and experimenting—with drugs, relationships, other cultures—but not with work! Casanova, Lord Byron, even Saint Francis of Assisi, and, more recently, socialites such as Alexis von Rosenberg, Paul Getty, and the Duchess of Windsor spent their youth traveling the world, studying in different cities, exploring different lifestyles and ideas, not settling down until their mid-20s or early 30s, and rarely financing their extended moratorium from their own funds. Thousands of sons, and even more daughters, of the European upper classes never entered an occupation or became economically independent of their parents, and few of them engaged in anything more consequential than developing new and sophisticated leisure lifestyles. Veblen (1899) detected this behavior emerging in history as early as in the ruling classes of primitive tribes, whom he christened the "leisure class."

There have always been emerging adults in the privileged sectors of cultures; the only difference is that today, because of growing affluence in the Western world, there are more of them around. Uncovering this "fact" is about as original as indicating that in richer societies there are more affluent people. Not even the heterogeneity of lifestyles in early adulthood on which Arnett remarks is a phenomenon of modern times. There have always been young people who were denied any period of playful moratorium in their growing-up years, while at the same time some of their rich contemporaries indulged in "accomplishing" themselves. At various historical times children under 10 years of age have worked in the mines and in the harvest fields, up chimneys, in city streets, in the army, the navy, and in factories, as housemaids, thieves, and prostitutes. In some cases, this early acceptance of adult status was not restricted to the poor. There have also been underage queens and kings, and very early arranged marriages within the nobility. The only thing that has changed in Western societies is that the backbreaking, manual jobs and escort "services" have now been transferred to the developing countries or are carried out by "imported" foreign workers.

These changes affecting the affluent world have been observed and commented on by researchers for some time. Three decades ago Winsborough (1978) analyzed trends in the United States regarding four adult transitions (work, school exit, military service, and first marriage) over the previous 30 years and found a time tendency toward later commencement of these transitions. In other words, the appearance of "delayed adulthood" was already in evidence in North America (at least) half a century before Arnett (2000) presented the scientific community with a term for describing this phenomenon.

Biological Changes and Emerging Adulthood

In Chapter 2 of this book, Tanner and Arnett make a powerful point from research into brain development, which in their view shows that "emerging adulthood corresponds with the final phase of organization of the adult brain."

On first impressions, this seems to make a convincing argument for this age period to be considered as a life phase leading to adulthood. On second thought, however, this conclusion is flawed because it is based on an oversimplified view of the human brain. There is never such a condition as the "final phase of the adult brain," because the brain itself is an ever-changing system, whose different areas undergo constant transformations across the entire life span. For example, metabolic activity in the brain first reaches adult levels in babies at the age of 10 months, and then exceeds it to peak around 4 years, when it gradually declines through childhood and adolescence, thereafter falling back to adult levels (Pinker, 1995). Gray matter density declines constantly over the dorsal frontal and parietal association cortices on both the lateral and interhemispheric surfaces, starting at the age of 7 years. However, in the left posterior temporal region, gray matter density increases continually until the age of 30 years, and then declines. Most of these changes seem to occur nonlinearly.

We can observe yet another pattern of brain activity in the cortex: the visual, auditory and limbic cortices show a linear pattern of ageing, whereas the frontal and parietal neocortices still develop in adulthood (Sowell et al., 2003), suggesting that development of the different areas of the cortex does not occur simultaneously (Giedd et al., 1999). Furthermore, although myelination develops very early in the life span in some areas of the brain (for example, the cingulated and primary visual cortices), in other areas it continues into old age (the posterior temporal lobes, Sowell et al., 2003). Similarly, each cell group of the hypothalamus has its own, sex-specific pattern of development, with some showing a dramatic decline with ageing and others becoming more active across the life span (Hofman, 1997). Without delving too deeply into corticoneurological research, it is easy to understand that even brain development is not a homogeneous, stage-like process, but a nonlinear process including gains and losses across different domains, just as in any other dynamic system.

Tanner and Arnett also list a wide range of competencies that seem to peak toward the end of emerging adulthood. Again, they select findings that support their theory, while ignoring others that reveal the "peaking" of abilities either at younger or older ages. For example, language learning circuitry in the brain is more plastic in childhood than at any other period of the life span, and the ability to learn phonology and grammar begins to decline after the age of 6 years (Pinker, 1995). Then bone healing ability declines from birth. For example, a femoral shaft fracture would heal within 3 weeks across childhood and adolescence; yet around 20 years, and then for many decades of adulthood, it will need 20 weeks on average to heal (Salter, 1998).

Furthermore, physiologically, peak aerobic capacity declines steadily from the age of 20 years (Flegg et al., 2005).

Cognitive-affective complexity also increases over the life span beyond young adulthood (Labouvie-Vief, DeVoe, & Bulka, 1989). Most practical abilities peak at mid-life (Schaie, 1983), the development of wisdom is unrelated to age (Baltes & Staudinger, 2000),[1] and, as Tanner and Arnett admit, fluid intelligence begins to decline during emerging adulthood, whereas chrystallized intelligence stabilizes. In other words, in some developmental areas emerging adults are still developing, in others they are stagnating, in some they have not begun to develop, and in others they have started to decline.

Tanner and Arnett quote Hershey and Farrell's (1999) finding that sometimes emerging adults show better task performance in practical everyday tasks than older adults. However, there is a vast body of research showing that "tacit knowledge" is mainly unrelated to age, but is dependent on experience (Sternberg et al., 2000). It is the demands and complexity of our occupation and the demands and support offered in our psychosocial and physical environment that develop expertise, reflective thinking, and performance independent of age (Fischer & Pruyne, 2003; Smith, Staudinger, & Baltes, 1994; Schooler, Mulatu, & Oates, 2004). Interestingly, these findings suggest that emerging adults who postpone engagement in demanding jobs might actually delay the development of these skills considerably. Importantly, neuroscience does not deny the significance of the environment for brain development, for example, in shaping synaptogenesis (Giedd et al., 1999). Once again, it is clear that human change and human development are better understood within a framework of dynamic processes than within a static stage theory.

Though Tanner and Arnett pay lip-service to the importance of environmental and cultural influences on the transitions to adulthood in the first part of Chapter 2, the sections on brain development consist exclusively of research conducted in the developed Western world. They even quote evidence from Perry (1970, 1981) to show that students' cognitive abilities increase in the time between entering and leaving college, claiming that such findings offer support for age-stage-related changes. Being university professors ourselves, we would hope that such changes are due to inputs, experiences, and influences other than brain maturation alone!

---

1 The only comment Baltes and Staudinger (2000) make about the relationship between age and wisdom is that "Ignoring the possibility of cohort effects, the major finding is that for the age range from about 25 to 75 years of age, the age gradient is zero." Tanner and Arnett interpret this finding as showing that the development of wisdom happens during emerging adulthood—we regard it as suggesting that there is *no correlation* between wisdom and age.

Psychosocial Considerations: Why Emerging Adulthood Is Not Necessarily a Positive Time

Relying on young people's own optimistic perspectives of their future lives, Arnett and Tanner (2006) present the period of emerging adulthood as a mainly positive experience for the individual not only in the United States but also in Europe (though Tanner and Arnett have revised their position on this substantially in Chapter 2, they reemphasize their rosy picture of the lifestyle of emerging adults in Chapter 3). Only recently, Arnett presented findings on the high levels of optimism of Danish university students, showing that they were similar in this to students in the United States. He regards this finding as supportive of his claim that optimism is a feature of all emerging adults because "Danes are hardly known for their sunny spirits" (Arnett, 2007a). Unfortunately for him (but fortunately for the Danes), he is wrong in making that assumption. For whatever reasons, Danes of all ages and social standing have been topping the "happiness league table" of the Eurobarometer (European Commission, 2007) for years.

For the rest of Europe, figures are not especially supportive of Arnett's hypothesis: 40% of 15–17 year olds expect that they will be worse off than their parents, and the parent generation is even less optimistic. On average, less than one European in five believes that the life of tomorrow's adults will be easier than that of adults today, whereas around two-third of Europeans believe life will be more difficult for the next generation (European Commission, 2007). The leading countries supporting this view are Germany, France, and Sweden, all of which are relatively wealthy nations.

There are also great differences in optimism depending on the age at which people left full-time education: 49% of those who stayed in full-time education until the age of 20 years or later believe their situation will improve, compared to 24% of those who left school at age 15 years or younger (European Commission, 2007). Such figures clearly reflect the gap between those whose education enhances future prospects and those who exit schooling before gaining qualifications. Furthermore, variations in optimism between countries are much larger than variations between age groups. Behind the average ratings, and for reasons far beyond the scope of this book, the number of those expecting their lives to get better in the future varies enormously between countries, from below 20% in Hungary, Germany, Austria, Belgium, and Bulgaria to around 50% in Estonia and the UK. Thus, the optimism that Arnett detected in his studies might well reflect the euphoria of the American (and Danish) way of life rather than a generalized optimism among young adults.

Arnett also makes the case that many studies show decreasing depression and increasing self-esteem in young people from their teens to mid-20s. However, this trend actually continues further along the life course, so that older adults are considerably less depressed than emerging adults (Kasen et al., 2003), indicating that the gradual decline in depression over the years has less to do with the leisurely lifestyle of some emerging adults than it has to do with the satisfactions associated with mastering the tasks of adulthood.

Equally interesting is the evidence that early adults are less happy today than they were generations ago. Data from birth cohort studies in the UK (Stewart & Vaitilingam, 2004) and the United States (Kasen et al., 2003) show that reported symptoms of depression and anxiety at age 24 years have doubled from the cohort born in 1958 to the cohort born in 1970. There is also a huge increase in reported unhappy relationships from one cohort to the other, as well as declining social attachments to the community, interest in politics, and a doubling of abstention from voting in elections. Most dissatisfied with their lives are single mothers, men still living in the parental home, and those in low-skilled jobs or without work. Note that three of these most discontented groups display the reported typical characteristics of emergent adults—not having committed to a career and still living at home.

Furthermore, Galambos, Barker, & Krahn (2006) found "being married" and "having fewer months in unemployment" to be powerful predictors of well-being in young adults. These data imply that those who already have attained the typical markers of adulthood and gained adult-like life experiences, such as leaving the parental home, finding a job, and getting married, are actually more contented than their age peers, who are still exploring and experimenting. In addition, regarding yourself as an adult as opposed to an emerging adult is also related to a higher sense of coherence (Luyckx, Schwartz, Goossens, & Pollock, 2008), healthier lifestyles (Blinn-Pike, Worthy, Jonkman, & Smith, 2008), less depression, and a higher sense of identity (Nelson & McNamara Barry, 2005). Hence, we dispute Arnett's claim that for most people the early 20s is a time of great well-being and supreme optimism.

We are joined in this scepticism by Twenge (2006), who describes the other side of increasing individualism and decreasing willingness to commit:

> One of the strangest things about modern life is the expectation that we will stand alone, negotiating breakups, moves, divorces, and all manner of heartbreak that previous generations were careful to avoid. This may be the key to the low rate of depression among older generations: despite all the deprivations and war they experienced, they could always count on each other. People had strong feelings

of community; they knew the same people all their lives; and they married young and stayed married. It may not have been exciting, and it stymied the dreams of many, but it was a stable life that avoided the melancholy that is so common now. (Twenge, 2006, p. 116)

Arnett describes the period of emerging adulthood not only as a period of optimism and of hopes for the future, but also as a period of insecurity. For some young people, these feelings of insecurity, anxiety, and hopelessness may offset any optimism they possessed. In extreme cases, these negative feelings are so powerful that young people choose to end their own life. The proportion of suicides committed by those between the ages of 5 and 45 years has increased from 44% in 1950 to 53% in 1995 (World Health Organization, 2002). Much of this growth has occurred among late adolescents and youth adults between the ages of 15 and 29 years. Suicide is currently among the top three causes of death for teenagers and young adults between the ages of 15 and 34 years in many countries (World Health Organization, 2001). As an example, although many young people in China see their future in optimistic terms, and consider their lives as "better than their parents," the suicide rate among them, particularly in females in rural areas, is one of the highest in the world (Hannum & Jihong, 2005; Nelson & Chen, 2007). Where expectations are high in a population, to perceive yourself as excluded from advancement may be difficult to accept.

On a societal level, Arnett (2007a) recognizes the phenomenon of emerging adulthood as a problem, because it causes falling birth rates, but at the same time he salutes it as "a beautiful problem," and "something wonderful, especially for emerging adults," on the grounds that affluent societies can afford the luxury of a largely unproductive, prolonged period of youth-moratorium. This is a rather naive analysis for two reasons. First, it is only a question of time before even the rich countries cannot afford this luxury. In Germany, for example, there is already such a lack of qualified engineers and technicians that the Government is being forced to change its immigration laws to be able to recruit a skilled work force from abroad (usually from countries that do not indulge extensive numbers of unproductive young adults). Additionally, in spite of these efforts, a shortfall of 330,000 academics is predicted by the year 2013 in Germany alone (Bonstein, 2008). Second, Arnett's analysis ignores the fact that the gap between rich and poor is expanding, not only within but also between countries. It is quite obvious that the affluence that makes emergent adulthood possible for some exists at the expense of those who do not have such choices. State benefits for unemployed youths or young carers are ridiculously low, compared to Government funding for university students

(Osgood et al., 2005), and if we add in the role of child labor and starvation in the Third World in creating these "beautiful problems" in the First World (see, for example, Bush, 2006), we can see the ethnocentricity of Arnett's analysis.

Why Arnett and Tanner Miss the Point Altogether

In the opening of Chapter 3, Arnett and Tanner state that our main criticism of Arnett's theory is that it does not take account of social class. Although it is true, as Schoon (2006) and others have stated, that Arnett has ignored the power of social class differences and painted a far-too-rosy picture of emerging adulthood, we have never made such a point specifically.

We have simply used social class on occasions as an example of the many variables that can influence the individual experience of the transitions to adulthood in order to illustrate that a universal age stage such as emerging adulthood is not feasible. Because of the plethora of possible influences and turning points in their lives, there are no two individuals who experience this transitional period in exactly the same way. Apart from the obvious mediator variables such as social class, gender, culture, ethnicity, income, educational attainment, and health, there are *many* others including relationship to parents, siblings, and mentors, friends, unemployment rates, labor market opportunities, skill-level and qualifications, governmental policies, and timing of life events and "twists of fate," such as meeting the "right or wrong" person at a decisive point in life. We agree completely with Arnett and Tanner that this is equally true at other times in the life course such as adolescence, which is why we have repeatedly argued that *any* stage theory of human development is insufficient to account for the processes and mechanisms involved.

The case studies described in Chapters 3 and 5 show with great clarity that it is neither age nor social class alone that is shaping these peoples' lives, but their own personal experiences and nonnormative shifts, such as unplanned pregnancies, drug addiction, lack of education, the possession of special skills, having to care for an incapacitated family member, social support, and unemployment. These are all factors that can impinge on our journey through life, and are very likely to cause a period of "identity moratorium" at any point in the life course. And it is these significant factors alongside with smaller day-to-day events, their timing in life (Elder & Shanahan, 2006), the range of resources an individual has to cope with them, and their complicated interaction and interplay that catalyze human change. Putting it all down to the emergence of a new age stage is a serious oversimplification that is unlikely to advance ideas and explanations within developmental psychology.

Why Stage Theories Do Not Work

The extensive heterogeneity of pathways to adulthood both within highly industrialised societies and across the globe is the one aspect of Arnett's argument with which we agree completely. As we said in Chapter 5, historically, when most members in the various sectors of a society had a very similar lifestyle because there were only a limited number of ways to survive, there were many more normative shifts, which all members of that particular society shared. These made them similar to each other in their life transitions. Thus, during these times, age was a reasonable predictor for their transformations across the life course.

Even when ways of life diversified with increasing industrialization and on into the twentieth century, heterogeneity did not pose a particular problem for psychologists because their research and findings were based on white, male, middle-class samples in the (rich Western) countries from which the researchers came. In this context, stage theories were relevant and useful. Ariès (1962) described the invention of childhood at the beginning of the nineteenth century, and then Hall (1904) created the notion of adolescence, followed by other stage theories, which all seemed to have a sound explanatory value. For example, there were Erikson's (1959) predictions about an identity crisis in adolescence, Levinson's (1978) ideas about the "season of early adult transitions" between 17 and 22 years of age, and Chickering and Havighurst's (1981) developmental task of achieving emotional independence between 16 and 23 years. All these theories were fairly useful and accurate interpretations of young, white, middle-class Americans in the mid-decades of the twentieth century.

Societies changed further as the twentieth century reached its last few decades and as the new millennium began, the life course has become destandardized and individualized (Beck, 1992). In turn, psychology has also changed over the years as it gained global recognition as a social science discipline, produced researchers in many countries, and had journals publish findings from many lands. As a scientific discipline it now aspires to explain human development per se.

What we are arguing for here is that the heterogeneity of transitions that Arnett considers as one of the main reasons for introducing, interpreting, and theorizing about a new developmental stage is actually the key argument against having stage theories at all. As Fischer and Bidell (1998) have argued repeatedly, the aim should be to explain developmental variability instead of trying to explain it away. Age can no longer be a predictor for any transitions across the life span, either among young people or among senior citizens: age itself does not explain a single change in human life, not even death. Heterogeneity is not only a prevalent characteristic of the lifestyles of young people; there is considerable variation across the life span: people become parents at a young age, in middle age, and with the help of in vitro transcription (IVT), even in old age:

> Next time you visit the supermarket, you may encounter . . . newborn infants with their mothers who are aged fifteen and sixteen and newborn infants with mothers aged thirty-five to forty . . . You may encounter, in fact, grandparents in their early forties as well as parents in their sixties and seventies. (Fiske & Chiriboga, 1991, p. 286)

Once they are parents, they live alone, or with the parent of their children, with another partner of the same or opposite gender, who might be of the same age or 20 years younger or older, they might be employed, unemployed, self employed, retired, returned to education, or embarking on a radical career shift, stay forever in their home town or move around the world—or any combination of these life choices. In recognizing this destandardization of the life course, the social sciences have progressed from the idea of stages toward systemic theories in order to begin to truly understand the mechanisms of human development:

> Adult life, then, is a process—a process, we must emphasise, which need not involve a predetermined series of stages of growth. The stages or hurdles which are placed in front of people and the barriers through which they have to pass (age-specific transitions) can be shifted around and even discarded. (Featherstone & Hepworth, 1991, p. 375)

A number of leading international academics have been significant contributors to this approach over the past few decades. These have included Bronfenbrenner's (1979; Bronfenbrenner & Morris, 1998) interactive microlevel to macrolevel theory, Elder's (1974) emphasis on both historical time and the timing of life events in the individual's development, Lerner's (1985, 1998) views on the importance of the individual's proactivity and self-agency in the developmental process, Baltes' (1987; Baltes, Lindenberger, & Staudinger, 1997) concepts of multidirectionality, plasticity, and the maximization of gains and the minimization of losses, as well as Valsiner's (1997) explorations of systemic developmental changes; we fully endorse the following quote, describing this innovative and illuminative development within the discipline:

> It was during the latter half of the 20th century that human developmentalists began to articulate a disciplinary understanding of the interrelatedness of form and function, structure and content, person and context, real time and developmental time, that challenged the classical developmental narratives of a discipline that was somewhat newly created . . . .. Development can be understood as a complex of multilevel, systemically nested, dialectical processes of organism-context relations. (the organismic-contextualist hypothesis can be found probably long before Marx, Einstein, Freud and Piaget) . . . .. This shift is not so pervasive as to be labelled a scientific revolution, but it does indicate a significant change in perspective among some developmental theorists and researchers. (Sorell, SoRelle-Miner, & Pause, 2007, p. 163)

In other words, we do not think that the solution to the difficulties in explaining increasingly diverse transitional pathways across the life span is by inserting yet another new stage into old theories, but that it is time to

> move away from a blanket categorisation of individuals in terms of stages bounded by chronological age towards a broader conception based on a range of trajectories or pathways. (Bynner, 2005, p. 378)

To conclude, we humbly submit that it has become necessary to accept that explanations of human change are somewhat more complicated today than assumed by the fathers of developmental psychology at a time of greater societal stability, and thus we require more sophisticated, multileveled theoretical models to explain development and gain an "understanding of the interrelatedness of form and function, structure and content, person and context, real time and developmental time" as Sorrell et al. (2007) have proposed.

7

In Defense of Emerging Adulthood as a Life Stage: Rejoinder to Kloep's and Hendry's Chapters 4 and 5

Jeffrey Jensen Arnett and Jennifer L. Tanner

In this chapter we present a response to the arguments made by Kloep and Hendry in Chapters 4 and 5. The central argument of Chapter 4 is that life stages in general, and the emerging adulthood (EA) stage in particular, are not helpful for understanding human development. Chapter 5 continues in this vein, but also emphasizes the diversity of developmental contexts with respect to culture, history, socioeconomic status, and gender, arguing that this diversity makes stage theories—including the theory of emerging adulthood—simplistic and inapplicable. Here we explain our alternative to their perspectives in both chapters, while also noting areas of agreement.

Emerging Adulthood as a Life Stage: Useful or Useless?

Kloep and Hendry argue that there is little to be gained from embracing the proposal that emerging adulthood is a new life stage that has developed in industrialized societies over the past half century. In fact, it is not just emerging adulthood they object to but all stage theories:

> [I]t is useless to describe human transitions as "stages" because in our "movement" through the life course we are advancing, regressing, developing in some domains and not others; in a sense ever-becoming but never arriving! Thus, conceptualizing stages only provides a simplistic description of broad life-phases and does not allow us to grasp the complexities of different transitions, processes and underlying, operational mechanisms. (p. 54)

We understand their concerns about the limitations of stage theories. It is a concern that has been expressed by many others as well (e.g., Elder & Shanahan, 2006; Thelen & Baltes, 2003). Kloep and Hendry's critique can be seen as part of a general backlash against stages in recent theorizing about human development (Lerner, 2002, 2006).

Stage theories were popular for most of the twentieth century. Freud's was the first, at the outset of the twentieth century, postulating a series of psychosexual stages of childhood, from oral to anal to oedipal to genital. In the 1930s Piaget proposed a stage theory of cognitive development from infancy through adolescence, and a stage theory of moral development in childhood. At mid-century Erikson took up Freud's idea and transformed the psycho-sexual stages to psychosocial stages, extending not just through childhood but through the entire life span. In the 1960s Kohlberg followed in Piaget's wake to form a more elaborate stage theory of moral development extending beyond childhood through adolescence. In the 1970s Daniel Levinson and his colleagues proposed a stage theory of adult development. Together, these stage theories dominated developmental psychology for most of the twentieth century.

However, in the waning decades of the twentieth century, stage theories began to fall out of favor (Lerner, 2002). Critics argued that the theories had overreached. These stage theories were grand, ambitious theories. They proposed a universal, ontogenetic program of development, even though the theories were based on limited, local samples—for Freud, a small number of upper class Jews in Vienna, mainly women; for Piaget, his own three children for his cognitive theory, and a handful of Swiss boys for his theory of moral development; for Erikson, his limited experience as a child psychologist and ethnographer; for Kohlberg, a small sample of boys in Chicago; for Levinson and colleagues, a small number of midlife adults from a handful of professions, all men. Yet on the basis of these tiny slices of humanity, the stage theorists ventured to propose their theories as true for all people in all places and times. Today this seems obviously untenable, and in retrospect it is surprising that the theories were able to dominate psychology for so long based on such limited data.

Another key objection to the grand stage theories was that they gave too little attention to the contexts of development (Lerner, 2006). In all twentieth century stage theories, development was believed to be driven by an ontogenetic program within the individual, with relatively little attention given to environmental contexts such as family, peers, school, and culture. In the waning decades of the twentieth century, developmental psychology rejected this view and turned instead to an elucidation of the contexts of development.

In addition to contexts, developmental psychology in recent decades has focused on general processes of development that apply across age periods (Baltes, Lindenberger, & Staudinger, 2006). Kloep and Hendry join their argument to this trend in Chapter 4, in advocating a "systemic perspective": "What makes a systemic perspective different from traditional views of development is that it abandons the idea of simple, unidirectional and linear processes of cause and effect in explaining change. Instead, it sees nature as an open system that both consists of, and belongs to, a number of other open systems; and as human beings, we are part of this natural configuration" (p. 58).

Let us be clear that we fully agree with the criticisms of the grand stage theories (see Arnett & Tanner, 2009). It was a mistake for those theorists to assert that their theories applied to all people in all places and times, especially based on such limited information. It was mistake for them to give so little attention to the contexts of development.

We have certainly sought to specify from the outset that emerging adulthood is not a theory that applies to all people in all places and times, but to young people in industrialized countries and to the growing middle class in developing countries (Arnett, 2000, 2002, 2006a, 2006b, 2007a, 2007b, 2010). We have also emphasized from the beginning the importance of considering multiple contexts for a complete understanding of emerging adulthood, including culture, history, social class, gender, and ethnicity, as well as family, school, and work contexts (Arnett, 2000, 2004, 2007a, 2007b, 2010).

Arnett initially avoided the term "stage" in presenting the theory of emerging adulthood, out of an awareness of the baggage the term had accumulated over the decades, and to avoid having the theory of emerging adulthood misconstrued as making universal and ontogenetic claims (Arnett, 2000). Instead, he described emerging adulthood as a new "period" of the life course. More recently, however, we have reconsidered this issue (Arnett & Tanner, 2009). Why should the use of "stage" be proscribed for all time because it was misused in developmental psychology in the twentieth century? Kloep and Hendry declare that all stages and all stage theories, including the theory of emerging adulthood, are "useless," but we believe stage theories can be useful and that there are good reasons to describe emerging adulthood as a new life stage.

As we see it, the function of any theory, including stage theories, is to assemble existing information in an original way that leads to new insights and new research. Even the twentieth century stage theories, for all their limitations, served that function well. The usefulness of the theory of emerging adulthood can be seen in how it has inspired thinking and research on this age period in the decade since it was first proposed. According to Google Scholar, Arnett's article in *American Psychologist* in 2000 has been cited over 1700 times (as of September 2010). Searches of PsycNet using "emerging adults" or "emerging adulthood" as search terms now yield hundreds of articles, books, and book chapters. And that is just in psychology. The theory of emerging adulthood has now been embraced and applied in many fields outside of psychology. A Google search of "arnett emerging adulthood theory" yielded 22,200 items in September 2010. At the four conferences on emerging adulthood that have been held so far a remarkable range of disciplines has been represented, including psychology, psychiatry, sociology, anthropology, education, epidemiology, health sciences, human development, geography, nursing, social work, philosophy, pediatrics, family studies, journalism, and law. Emerging adulthood has flourished because thousands of scholars around the world, across a wide range of disciplines, independently read about the theory and concluded that it is useful and that they can use it to illuminate what they have seen in their research and in their personal experience.

The key question for any theory should be, does it inspire new knowledge and research? That is, does it guide our thinking in new ways that improve our understanding? For emerging adulthood, the answer is unequivocally yes. Consider how little research attention the age period from the late teens through the 20s has received in the past. Developmental psychology has focused mainly on infancy and early childhood, with attention dwindling by adolescence and then petering out altogether thereafter. Social psychology has made abundant use of university students in their late teens and early 20s, but only as supposed representatives of all adults, rarely with a consideration of the distinctive developmental characteristics of their age group. Sociology has focused mainly on transition events in this age period, such as leaving home, finishing education, marriage, and entering parenthood. Attention to the developmental issues of the age period from the late teens through the 20s has been scarce.

The theory of emerging adulthood has contributed to a boom in research on this age period over the past decade. The value of the theory of emerging adulthood is that it leads us to investigate a wide range of questions about the developmental characteristics of this new life stage. How does leaving home influence relations with parents? For emerging adults who remain home or return home, how do relations with parents change or remain the same? What place do friends have in the lives of emerging adults? Do they matter more than in adolescence, because emerging adults have often moved away from home, or less, because emerging adults are no longer in the daily peer-rich environment of secondary school? How do emerging adults make and break romantic partnerships, and how do they view sexuality and marriage in an era of widespread premarital sex and cohabitation? What kinds of media are important in the daily lives of emerging adults and how does media use inhibit or enhance their social relations? These are the kinds of questions that the theory of emerging adulthood is inspiring.

These questions are new because the life stage of emerging adulthood is new. The extension of education and the later ages of entering marriage and parenthood make the years of the late teens through the 20s different than they have been in the past. For most people in industrialized societies, ages 18–25 (at least) are years not of settling into adult roles in love and work but the most unsettled years of the life span, when changes are rapid and it is difficult to predict what life will be like 5 years later. Consequently, what is happening during these years with respect to family relationships, peer relations, romantic relationships, self-development, education, and work is likely to be considerably different than it was in adolescence or it will be in the more settled years of young adulthood that will follow for most people.

It is not enough simply to focus on "systemic processes" as if life stages are irrelevant. In statements about systems and processes, the language quickly becomes abstract and disconnected from the reality of how people live, as in this statement by Kloep and Hendry from Chapter 4:

> New resources are added, others disappear, some characteristics become resources, and some lose their resourceful quality . . . What we are really analyzing is not resources on one hand and challenges on the other, but the relationship between the two. (p. 66, 68)

Fine, but wouldn't it be more useful to connect this specifically to life stages and ask, for example, what resources are added and lost from adolescence to emerging adulthood to young adulthood, and what challenges are most likely to be characteristic of each life stage? Indeed, without an anchor in specific life stages, statements about systems and processes have limited use-fulness in understanding human development, in our view. It is difficult to see what research might be inspired by a statement such as Hendry's and Kloep's unless it were applied to a specific life stage.

Kloep and Hendry themselves validate the usefulness of thinking of devel-opment in terms of life stages in their chapters. Although they go on about "resource systems" as a general principle of development in Chapter 4, this remains an abstraction and it is unclear how it can be used to understand development. However, the chapter becomes more vivid when they discuss normative, quasinormative, and nonnormative shifts and apply this idea spe-cifically to the emerging adult years. They mention obvious quasinormative shifts—"experiences which are . . . common and socially expected to occur within a certain age-range in a given culture"—such as leaving the parental home and getting a first job, but this idea could be broadened to ask, what is the range of quasinormative shifts in emerging adulthood, and to what extent are there similarities and differences across cultures? Leaving the parental home in emerging adulthood is a quasinormative shift in Denmark but not in Italy. What quasinormative shifts might be distinctive to emerging adulthood in Italy? More generally, are there psychological quasinormative shifts in emerging adulthood, such as the five features proposed by Arnett (2004)—identity explorations, feeling in-between, and so on? The idea of quasinorma-tive shifts can be fruitful, but only if applied specifically to life stages. This illustrates the value of stages, including emerging adulthood.

Ultimately, it is nearly impossible to understand human development without invoking life stages in some form. Development is change over time, from one age period to the next, and to communicate about development it is necessary to refer to life stages and the developmental characteristics they represent—infancy, childhood, adolescence, and yes, emerging adulthood. Here again, Kloep and Hendry provide evidence for our point of view. They resist the term "emerging adulthood," but they have to use some kind of term for the age period from the late teens through the 20s, they have to call it *some-thing*, so they often end up using "early adulthood." But this is a vague and unsatisfying term. Kloep and Hendry never explain what they mean by it, or what makes it superior to "emerging adulthood." In contrast, Arnett (2004, 2006a, 2006b) has explained in detail his reasons for proposing "emerging adulthood" and why he believes it is preferable to other terms. Scholars who wish to resurrect one of the previous terms as an alternative to emerging adulthood have an obligation to explain why it is preferable to emerging adult-hood. So far, to our knowledge, no scholar has done so. Many sociologists use "early adulthood" or "young adulthood" or "youth," without ever defining or justifying these terms (e.g., Bynner, 2005; Heinz, 2009), and that includes Kloep and Hendry in this book.

Furthermore, in their scheme of the life course, Kloep and Hendry (2007), have "early adulthood" stretching from adolescence to middle adulthood. This makes little sense. The life of the typical 20 year old in industrialized societies—economically dependent on parents, still in education or training or looking for stable employment, unmarried, no children, uncertain about identity issues and about the form their adult life will take—is vastly different from the life of the typical 30 or 35 year old—economically independent, finished with education, in a long-term romantic partnership or marriage, at least one child, stable employment or full-time parenthood. Nothing is gained from calling the whole long dramatic diverse stretch of life from age 18 to 45 years "early adulthood." In fact, any single term for a stage of life so long and so different from the earlier to the later part of it is meaningless and—if we may so—useless. Since referring to life stages is essential for making sense of human development, let us at least use life stage terms and concepts that are coherent, clearly defined, and make conceptual sense.

Who Experiences Emerging Adulthood, and Who Does Not?

Kloep and Hendry devote most of Chapter 5 to an examination of the variability in the age period from the late teens to the late 20s, culturally, historically, and in terms of social class and educational attainment. They provide an interesting summary of the nature of the transition to adulthood in developing countries and in countries with different economic systems, including agricultural, mixed, and "postmodern" economies. Interesting, yes, but most of it is irrelevant to emerging adulthood theory. EA theory has never claimed to be universal, and it has been explicitly stated that it does not apply to developing countries except to the small (but growing) middle class in those countries (Arnett, 2000, 2007a, 2007b).

The social class objection comes up again, too, in their Chapter 5. That is, it is claimed again that emerging adulthood applies only to the "affluent middle classes" who receive extensive higher education. We can only reply, again, that EA theory is based on research with persons from a wide range of social class backgrounds and levels of educational attainment (e.g., Arnett, 2004), whereas the claim that the theory applies only to the "affluent middle classes" is typically made without proffering any evidence.

Kloep and Hendry do present evidence in their chapter in the form of case studies, so in our reply here we will examine their cases in relation to questions about EA theory. Our plan here is to use their own material as evidence in favor of our thesis (and against theirs). Most of their cases are outliers, people who have exceptional circumstances that make them unusual compared to others in their age group, but even the outliers have characteristics that support EA theory. The cases fall into three general types: normative, early entry to adult roles, and off-track.

Normative Cases: The Student and the Nanny

The student described by Kloep and Hendry represents fairly well the EA path of those who pursue university education, at least from what we can tell by his mother's account. He is an adult in some ways but not others. On the one hand, he has moved out of his family household and manages to take care of himself while at the university, so he clearly has moved beyond the dependency of adolescence. She recognizes this change in his development, noting that she now lets him come and go as he likes, rather than monitoring him closely as she did when he was younger.

On the other hand, he is clearly not fully adult in other ways. Although he manages quite well for himself when he is away, when he comes home his mother cooks meals for him, does his accumulated laundry, and takes him around where he needs to go. He accepts her doting but also resents it because "he likes his independence now." Like many emerging adults, he appears to feel ambivalent about reaching adulthood (Arnett, 1998, 2004), enjoying the freedom of it but less joyful about taking on for himself the dreary daily tasks of adult life such as doing laundry.

The nanny has embarked on quite a different path through emerging adulthood, but her case also has normative features. She is a live-in nanny and takes care of four children each day from 7 a.m. to 7 p.m. She calls herself an adult, and who could doubt her? Like those who have become parents at a young age, she considers her responsibilities for children to be an indisputable marker of adulthood (Arnett, 1998). Taking on responsibilities and making independent decisions are the top two criteria for her in marking adult status, as they are for so many other emerging adults, and she believes she has attained them (Arnett, 2003; Mayseless & Scharf, 2003).

She seems quite settled in terms of work, earlier than most of her peers. At age 18, she is happy with her work as a nanny and plans to be a "child minder" long into the future. Yet her life plan in terms of love is precisely normative: she plans to marry and have her first child between ages 25 and 30, as the majority of young people in industrialized countries do. Although she has no current boyfriend, she states with double hopefulness, "I hope I will find someone in the next 2 years hopefully."

Perhaps the most interesting part of the nanny's case is her experience of a "gap year" prior to her current job. The gap year is a year (sometimes two or three years) between secondary school and either settled work or entering university. It is said to be common in northern Europe, although to our knowledge there is not yet any systematic research on it. (A PsycNet search in February 2009 yielded not a single article on the topic.) Sometimes emerging adults use this time to try to figure out what to do next; sometimes they already know but want to wait before entering the next step in education or work. Some of them pursue leisure, travel, and adventure during this time while working at low-level jobs. The gap year is a classic experience of emerging adulthood, as it involves identity explorations and instability, and is highly self-focused. At no other time of life do people have this freedom to experiment with a range of different self-chosen experiences.

The young woman in this case study embarked on her gap year to be sure that a career in child care would be right for her. Like most other emerging adults, she was determined that her work would be more than a job, not just a way to make a living but "something that I enjoy." Her mother pressed her to go to university, but she resisted because her heart was really with child care. Nevertheless, to put this aspiration to an identity test, in her gap year she had "15 different jobs." She "hated them all," and returned to child care firm in the conviction that she had made the right choice. "Now I'm happy just to stick with child care, because I've got everything out of my system and I'm doing things the way I want."

Her case illustrates that non-college-emerging adults also look for identity-based work and that frequent changes in jobs during emerging adulthood can be part of work-related identity explorations (Arnett, 2004). It also highlights the fascinating and important phenomenon of the gap year, which invites serious research attention.

Entering Adulthood Early: The Young Mother and the Young Married Man

Although median ages of entering marriage and parenthood have risen all across the world in recent decades, some people still enter these transitions at an early age. Kloep and Hendry provide two examples in their case studies, a young mother and a young married man.

The young mother, age 20, sings the familiar refrain of young parents, that responsibilities for a child make them indisputably adult (Arnett, 1998). "I am an adult, because I have got a 2 year old child, so I've had to grow up a lot quicker than most teenagers did." As noted in Chapter 3, other emerging adults also invoke responsibility as the primary criterion of adulthood, but they usually specify that they mean responsibility for themselves, whereas for young parents it is responsibility for others, a key difference. "I've got responsibilities now, obviously, because I've got a daughter to look after, so it's not just me I've got to think about now."

As Arnett (1998) has discussed, having a child at a young age is a sudden, immediate entry into adulthood, in contrast to the gradual, incremental path that most emerging adults take. In many ways, emerging adulthood ends (or never begins) for a young mother when a child is born. Yet in other aspects of her life, this young mother sounds many of the themes of emerging adulthood rather than young adulthood. She still lives with her parents, and recognizes that as a dependent status. She needs her parents for financial support and for child care. "It's my mother really that I depend on, because she babysits a lot for me." She looks forward to moving out eventually, but admits "that could be a few years down the line."

In both love and work, she remains undecided and unsettled, a work in progress, like most other emerging adults. She has no current love partner, but is hopeful of finding one, perhaps through her current job as a shop clerk. "It's a way of meeting new people, so hopefully I'll meet my new man in my shop." She envisions the domestic life she one day hopes to have. "If I meet someone then we'll probably set up a home, which would be a nice thing to look forward to."

With regard to work, she likes her job in the shop well enough. "I like working in a shop, I enjoy it and it's a couple of hours out of the house." However, this kind of work is not what she had planned. She admits, "I chose not to go to university because of my daughter." Yet she still hopes to pursue identity-based work eventually. "I would like to work with children perhaps, I always said when I was in school that I'd like to be a teacher." Thus, even though she has a young child she resembles her emerging adult peers in that she is still very much in the process of building the structure of an adult life. It is just that with the responsibilities of parenthood, she has a much narrower scope for pursuing the kind of adult life she would like for herself.

Like the young mother, the young married man also entered a major adult role early, but for him it was planned. He simply met the love of his life earlier than most people do. "I met M and bang! I was in real love at the first sight, man! I talked to my mother, then to her parents and several months we were together, we got married." His wife is 3 years older than he is, and he admits that she was the driving force behind the early marriage. "It was her idea to marry so quickly. And I agreed." Because women usually marry about 2 years younger than men, on average, her marriage at age 23 was much closer to the norm than his marriage at age 20.

He seems settled in work as well as in love. He works as a "security tech" in a factory. "I watch the monitors and sometimes walk the perimeter and check if no one tries to steal our junk." Unskilled labor, to be sure, and hardly identity-based work; he admits it is "a bit boring." But he does not aspire to anything much different. He sees himself remaining in the security field, maybe moving eventually to a "high-profile place" where he would have "better money, better experience and better opportunities. And then, who knows?"

So, is he an emerging adult, or has he emerged early into young adulthood? It is difficult to say from the limited information available, but there are some interesting clues in his thoughtful observations on his status. He recognizes that he has attained two of the markers widely associated with adulthood. "I've got a job, I am married." But, like other emerging adults (Arnett, 1998, 2003), he doubts that these transitions really mean much as markers of adulthood. They did not seem to change his life much, he feels. "I still don't have my own house, and I have the same friends and interests I had before. So it wasn't any great change for me." He sees financial independence as one key to adult status, but admits "we live still with our parents," although they have plans to move into their own apartment within a month or two.

He is not sure he is fully adult, and he is not sure he wants to be. Like many emerging adults (Arnett, 2004), he is ambivalent about entering adulthood, because adulthood looks like the end of fun. "When you say 'adult' I imagine my parents and other people that are, say, forty now, but well . . . they seem boring. And many people I know never gave up the fun, they're the same people they were." For now, he certainly seems like he is still emerging. "I still feel young, very young."

Off-Track: The Unemployed, the Carers, and the Offender

Five of the cases presented by Kloep and Hendry are of young people who are in unusual circumstances that have taken them off track in their development through emerging adulthood. Two are unemployed, two are "carers" for ailing parents, and one is an offender.

Unemployment tends to be high in emerging adulthood, relative to other adult age groups. In most countries, the rate of "youth unemployment" (usually ages 15–24) is about twice as high as the overall unemployment rate (Wolbers, 2007). This is not surprising in light of the fact that young workers usually have fewer skills and less experience than older workers, making them less attractive to potential employers. Younger workers have also had less time than older workers to build social capital that leads to employment. Also, in emerging adulthood workers are more likely to be able to quit a job they don't like to search for a better one that is more identity based, with a period of unemployment in between. Unlike older workers, they usually do not yet have responsibilities for supporting others economically, and many have the option of living in their parents' household while they are between jobs.

For all emerging adults, making their way into the vast, complex, diverse world of adult work is challenging. Children no longer simply grow up to do whatever their fathers or mothers did. Now they have to find their own place in an immense array of possible jobs, and usually they are searching for a job that is more than a job, something that will be enjoyable and satisfying (Walther, 2009).

The two unemployed young men described in Kloep and Hendry's cases both seem overwhelmed by this challenge. The mother of the 18-year-old man describes him as being afflicted with a "lack of motivation, lack of concentration, he can't really be bothered to do things, he doesn't want to get out of bed in the morning and when he does get up, all he wants to do is just lounge about in the front room and watch the telly." Like many other emerging adults, he seems ambivalent about taking on adult responsibilities, not just in work but in other ways, according to her. "I still look after him, do his washing, ironing, cooking, cleaning, picking up after him sometimes, and just generally doing things that I've always done for him more or less. It's still the same as when he was a child. He thinks he's an adult, but he's not, when it comes to going to the hospital, or dentist or something, its 'MUM—come with me' so . . . he's still my baby boy really."

The 16-year-old unemployed young man seems similarly daunted and confused by the challenges of entering the adult work world. Like the 18-year-old young man, he seems to be wrestling with identity issues and losing, so far. "Everybody thinks they know me, but do they hell! I don't even know me, so there's bound to be summat good in me somewhere." Yet he broods over his identity and fears that there may not be "summat good" within him after all. "I think a lot, about me and how c**p things are. I think they're gonna try me on one of these alternative education programme things—it won't be much use though 'cos I'm not good at it, see." But he is only 16 years old, still more adolescent than emerging adult, so it could be that he is just now taking his first hesitant steps toward forming an adult work identity.

The two carers are highly unusual and interesting cases. The 17-year-old carer takes care of her parents, who have "serious mental illness." She is clearly unable to pursue a normal emerging adulthood, but what is interesting about her account is how she realizes, with regret, that her identity options have been foreclosed by her responsibilities for her parents. "I would like to be a nursery nurse, but mam and dad have to be my priority. When I was younger I had all these great ideas about being a teacher . . . It's all just made me lose interest in me. I don't know what I would do if I wasn't a carer, 'cos—that's me now, it's who I am." She has identity aspirations similar to other emerging adults, but without the freedom to pursue them, which leaves her frustrated and despondent.

The other carer, an 18-year-old man, sounds similar themes. He takes care of a brother and a mother who are mentally ill. Like the 17-year-old carer, he realizes and laments that he has not been able to pursue a normal course of identity explorations in emerging adulthood. "It's been ages since I did what I enjoyed—years! I would like to have some time to experiment and find me. But it's not going to happen, and I'd feel too guilty. I love my family, but I'm scared of having to do this forever." For both carers, their regrets over their circumstances reflect an implicit cultural awareness that in the UK it is normative in emerging adulthood to pursue identity explorations and that they are missing out.

For the young offender, too, there is an awareness of being in the time of life when identity issues are central, and being prevented by individual circumstances from following the normative route. "I haven't got a lot going for me and no real ideas about what to do," he admits. He imagines how his life could be different, better, if he could make progress in his identity development. "If I could find something I'm good at . . . If I could ever find a talent, then I could feel a bit better about myself." But he sees this as unlikely ever to happen. He fears he has discovered his true self and that it is no good. "I expect to get stuff wrong, and got no faith in what I'm like. I reckon 'cos if I let people know me I might not like what they see, 'cos not many would stick around with me." With the stigma of a criminal record, he despairs that the die of his life is cast. "A kid with a track record like mine don't get nobody interested in . . . I know what I am . . . but I can't change it but no matter what."

Conclusion: The Value of the Emerging Adulthood Framework

Emerging adulthood is perhaps the most diverse of all life stages, when little is normative, and it is important always to keep this heterogeneity in mind when considering its developmental features. Nevertheless, it is striking how identity issues rise persistently to the top in emerging adults' discussions of their lives. For many and perhaps most emerging adults, the primary developmental task of this life stage is to clarify an identity and find a fit between their identity and the possibilities available to them in the adult world they will soon enter. Where those possibilities are constricted or cut off, emerging adults feel the frustration of lacking what they believe others their age have.

We believe the emerging adulthood framework helps make sense of what happens developmentally during the age period from the late teens to the late 20s, even for the nonnormative cases presented by Kloep and Hendry. They prefer to focus on processes and avoid conceptualizing development in terms of life stages. No doubt both perspectives have value, just as both perspectives have their advocates: to each his or her own, in pursuit of greater understanding of this fascinating age period.

8

Bringing Down the Curtain

Jeffrey Jensen Arnett, Marion Kloep, Leo B. Hendry, and Jennifer L. Tanner

In this last chapter, all four authors will comment on how, if at all, it might be possible to reconcile the different standpoints of stage and ecological theory. All views are presented independently by each of the authors in turn, so there may be some repeated themes within the four sections. This book aimed to be an invitation to an open debate, something that is rare among scholars today, but something that we think is absolutely necessary to drive forward research and theory building (and on this one point, the four of us agree wholeheartedly!). We hope in the previous chapters of our book that we have given examples of how such a debate could further our never-ending endeavors to understand the fascinating course of human development.

Part I: Jeffrey Jensen Arnett: One Stage, Many Paths

In this final chapter, we agreed that we would each seek to find some common ground between our two camps. This is easy enough to do, at least from our end. We have no objection to Kloep and Hendry's insistence that there are processes of development that apply across age periods. Furthermore, we see no reason why an examination of processes would preclude the use of age-based stages, including emerging adulthood. Why not use both, toward a complete understanding of human development? Where they go wrong, in our view, is in viewing processes and stages as mutually exclusive. We hope that the exchange in the chapters of this book has moved them toward seeing the utility of stages, including emerging adulthood—or, if not Kloep and Hendry, perhaps readers of the book.

The goal of our investigations of human development, according to Kloep and Hendry, should be to identify universal processes of human development, applying to all people in all places and times. After all, they argue, this is what the natural sciences have achieved, and "Why should the social sciences be satisfied with less?" (p. 110). But it is precisely this analogy of with the natural sciences, this "physics envy," as it has been called, that has run the social sciences off course during their short history. Because human cultures are marvelously diverse, studying human beings is not like studying other animals, and it is certainly not like studying natural laws. The second law of thermodynamics is the same in Scotland as in Japan, but the way of life that humans have developed in Scotland is much different than the way of life developed by the Japanese. Stripping away cultural distinctiveness in pursuit of human universals was the great error of psychology in the twentieth century (Arnett, 2008).

This does not mean that there is no need to take into account human characteristics and tendencies that provide the raw material for development across cultures. We hold with Richard Shweder's proposal that cultural psychology should involve the investigation of "one mind, many mentalities" (Shweder et al., 2006, p. 865). That is, there are features of cognitive functioning that are part of being human in all places and times, but these features are stamped with distinctive forms or "mentalities" in different cultures. For emerging adulthood, we would revise this to "one stage, many paths." That is, the demographic patterns that have led to the rise of a new life stage of emerging adulthood are the same worldwide—longer education and higher ages of entering marriage and parenthood—but the paths taken through this new stage vary widely both within and between cultures (Arnett, 2010).

Kloep and Hendry claim that the theory of emerging adulthood is not really a theory at all because it "neither adds explanation nor prediction" (p. 110). We dispute this, and we believe the hundreds (if not thousands) of scholars worldwide now using the emerging adulthood paradigm would dispute it as well. The theory explains why the demographic patterns that frame emerging adulthood have taken place, locating them in economic changes away from manufacturing and toward information and technology, which requires more extensive postsecondary education and training, and in social changes, especially changes in women's roles and greater acceptance (or at least tolerance) of premarital sex (Arnett, 1998, 2004). Some predictions of the theory have been tested in the decade since the theory was first proposed, most notably the prediction that persons in the 18- to 25-year-old age period would typically describe themselves as neither adolescent nor adult but in-between, adults in some ways but not others. This finding has now been reported in diverse countries, as described in earlier chapters of this book.

Another key prediction of the theory is that emerging adulthood will continue to spread as a new life stage in the decades to come, as countries worldwide reach a level of economic development and integration into the global economy that will make emerging adulthood possible (Arnett, 2006b, 2007b). The veracity of this prediction remains to be seen, but fascinating evidence in support of it is already coming out. One recent example is Leslie Chang's book *Factory Girls*, about young women in China who are migrating from rural villages to urban areas in search of jobs in China's rapidly expanding economy (Chang, 2008). The women typically begin by working at a factory job they obtained through a friend or family member, but soon they become more aware of the range of jobs available in their new urban location, and they switch jobs frequently in search of more satisfying and financially rewarding work. They seek out further education and training to enhance their job skills so that they can compete for better-paying jobs. They make and break romantic relationships of their own choosing, rather than accepting a marriage arranged by their parents back in the village. They dream of finding true love and satisfying work and of making enough money to live well. In short, their lives look remarkably similar in many ways to the lives of emerging adults in economically developed countries, yet vastly different than the lives of their parents and peers who remained in the village.

Another criticism by Kloep and Hendry is that the theory of emerging adulthood "will almost certainly become outdated, since Western societies are bound to change and new cohorts emerge with different developmental characteristics in different social contexts" (p. 110). Here again we find a point of agreement. Another mistake of twentieth century developmental theories was their claim to be theories for all time. No theory of human development lasts forever, because humans are cultural creatures, and cultures inevitably change over time. Theories are useful as frameworks of understanding. They help us make sense of what we know, direct our attention to promising areas of inquiry, and interpret the results of our investigations and observations. We believe the theory of emerging adulthood currently serves this function well. When it ceases to do so, it will be superseded by another theory that is more useful. But for now, and for as far into the future as the eye and imagination can see, the theory of emerging adulthood will be fruitful as a way of understanding young people's development in economically developed countries, and it can be expected to be useful in the century to come as a way of predicting and explaining the changes occurring in the lives of an increasing proportion of young people in developing countries.

Although we believe that all theories are mortal, we disagree with Kloep and Hendry's position that age-based theories are already obsolete: "Age can no longer be a predictor for any transitions across the life span, either among young people or among senior citizens: age itself does not explain a single change in human life, not even death. Heterogeneity is not only a prevalent characteristic of the lifestyles of young people, there is considerable variation across the lifespan" (p. 119). The fact that "there is considerable variation across the life span" in each age period does not mean that "Age can no longer be a predictor for any transitions across the life span." Here Kloep and Hendry take what we regard as an extreme position. Of course age can be a predictor for life transitions. Infants who are 12 months old can be predicted to walk soon. Toddlers who are 2 years old can be predicted to be talking soon in complete sentences. Girls and boys who are 10 years old can be predicted to undergo the changes of puberty within the next few years.

The changes of emerging adulthood are less predictable because it is a culturally based life stage, not a biological one. Still, it may be fruitful to entertain and investigate questions about what is predictable during emerging adulthood, and in what contexts. To what extent and in which cultural contexts can it be predicted that emerging adults will move out of their parents' household? To what extent and in which cultural contexts can it predicted that emerging adults will obtain postsecondary education or training? To what extent and in which cultural contexts can it be predicted that emerging adults will experience their time of life as an age of identity explorations, an age of instability, a self-focused age, an age of feeling in-between, and an age of possibilities? These are examples of the kinds of promising research questions that can be generated by taking age seriously as a potential predictor of developmental changes.

This has been an enjoyable and fruitful exchange with our colleagues Marion Kloep and Leo Hendry. They have served as foils but also as partners in pursuing a greater understanding of emerging adulthood, and we have learned much from their perspective. We hope this book can serve as an example of what has been called "adversarial collaboration" (Kahneman, 2003). Academic disputes all too often become personal battles, characterized by *ad hominem* attacks and recriminations. Here, we have shown that scholars who have markedly different views can engage in vigorous debate, and still share a laugh and raise a glass together afterward.

Part II: Marion Kloep: What We Can Learn from Polar Bears:
Changing a Stage or Staging a Change?

Following all the points that have been made throughout the book, I want to
reiterate that Arnett's concept of emerging adulthood is not a theory, but merely
an observation. Let me explain that with an analogy: some years ago, scientists
observed that the ice at the polar caps is melting. Now, nobody would have
proclaimed this as a new theory about the physical properties of water. It was
just a description of a natural phenomenon. To understand this phenomenon,
we need more than a description. For example, we need to know the physical
rules of the interdependence between temperature and the physical state
of water, and, to go further, the role of solar activity, volcanic eruptions, and
greenhouse gases, and so on in the ecological system. In other words, we need
a theory to explain and hopefully give guidelines on how to exert some control
over these phenomena. Now, the observation that the behavior of young people
under certain circumstances has changed does not explain anything.

Does being an observation rather than a theory render Arnett's concept
worthless? Not at all. First, the very inadequacy of the concept as a theory forces
developmental scientists to offer an alternative that is capable of explanation—
and we have made one of these attempts in this book. Changing old stage theories by inserting a new stage might well have been an important step toward
creating a more radical change, namely, abolishing stage theories altogether.
That way, Arnett might still have rendered an important contribution to theory
development within psychology.

Second, and closely linked to this argument, if nobody had observed the
melting ice at the poles, nobody would have come up with theories to explain it.
All theories begin with observation. Though not being the first to observe it,
Arnett is without doubt one of the most powerful disseminators of the fact
that the lifestyles of some young adults have changed compared to earlier generations. Apart from forcing scientists to come up with explanations, this
awareness also has policy implications. In the same way as politicians all over
the world congregate and discuss how to meet the challenges of global warming (even though scientists have not yet agreed on an undisputed theory to
explain it!), institutions that work with young people should be aware that they
are dealing with individuals who have characteristics and values different than
what was prevalent some decades ago. For example, the media are full of complaints that students' attitudes and behavior are different from those of earlier
generations. Present-day students are accused of being less independent and
less interested in academic issues, and their academic performance is worse

than that of former cohorts (e.g. Newman, 2008). Complaints, however, will not change the issue—though being aware that young people have changed and how they have changed (whereas universities have not) could be the start of a solution to the issue. Another example is that the government of the UK seems oblivious to the fact that the situation of school-alienated teenagers has altered with the changing economic situation and the limited availability of unskilled labor. Blind to the needs of this growing number of young people neither in work nor in education, they try to solve the problem with an outdated solution by forcing them to remain within the compulsorily education system for a longer period of time. Being more aware of the ways the transitions into adulthood have changed might be a starting point for formulating more effective strategies.

Third, our differences with Arnett might be partly caused by the standpoint of the observer. The polar bear on his melting ice-flow is completely unaware of theories of global warming or even the effect of temperature on water, and anyway, theories would be of no help to him in his situation. However, (if he could think and plan) he might want to know that he is facing a problem that is more than temporary, and that he shares it with the rest of his species, so that he might reconsider his lifestyle and hunting techniques. Similarly, to know that their situation is not unique can add to young peoples' self-understanding, and to know what they can expect from the future can increase their self-agency. For example, parents no longer consider a delay in launching their young adults into the world as a personal failure, knowing that the age of leaving the parental home is rising everywhere.

Fourth, and most importantly, Arnett's concept contains some highly interesting observations that may well be the starting point for a whole new era of research. These observations, however, have nothing to do either with new stages or with emerging adulthood. Much more interesting than these are the features that allegedly characterize this period, namely, a time of uncertainty, a time of possibilities, a time of self-centeredness, and a time of identity exploration. These are not shifts in themselves, but rather the consequences of shifts in one's life, and they all describe experiences that increasing numbers of people recognize as their own—but these experiences are *not* bound to a certain age range. As our own research with retired people has shown (Kloep & Hendry, 2007), it is not only emerging adults who go through periods in which they do not have a secure identity, do not know how to reinvent themselves, and cannot decide what to commit to in terms of occupation, partnership, values, and independence. These periods characterize recurring moratoria that many individuals experience as a consequence of significant life changes during their life course—whereas others tackle the inherent challenges by choosing to ignore them.

Now, knowing that there are some young, middle-aged and older individuals who may or may not experience identity foreclosure, diffusion, or moratorium when faced with certain challenges (such as starting a job or leaving a job) immediately raises the question of what processes and mechanisms are responsible for individuals acting so differently from each other. The age stage they happen to be in hardly contributes to understanding individual differences. For instance, becoming a parent for the first time can now happen anytime between 13 and 80 years of age. So age neither explains the challenge nor the identity processes that occur as a response (new identities are constructed across the whole life span). Tanner (2006) comes close to touching on this point in writing the following: "Teasing apart the role of context in emerging adulthood from the characteristics of the age period is important" (p. 43). She also sees the need for taking into consideration variables other than the immediate environment surrounding a person, suggesting that "Together, differences in starting points before emerging adulthood as well as experiences during emerging adulthood interact to increase the spread between those who go into emerging adulthood more or less advantaged" (p. 47). Take "emerging adulthood" out of this quotation and replace it with a non-age-limited term such as "transitional periods" and there is nothing I could disagree with!

In other words, for us as developmental scientists, it would be fascinating to research the factors that make people of whatever age enter a period of moratorium (and find themselves feeling exactly as Arnett's emerging adults). We have offered a tentative answer to this in suggesting that it may be a combination of important challenges in their lives, the psychosocial resources an individual can fall back on (a point that Tanner, 2006, obviously agrees with!), together with the ecological interactions of various life span variables that account for the individual differences in people's development. To put it briefly, lose the constrictions of an age-bound stage, and instead investigate the processes and mechanisms of human diversity in reacting to life's infinite challenges, and I might even join forces with Tanner and Arnett in staging a change!

Part III: Leo B. Hendry: "As John McEnroe Used to Say . . ."

For some strange reason, whenever I read what Arnett and Tanner have written in this book or when I consider other publications of Arnett's, I always think of tennis! So what I would like to do in this section allotted to me in the concluding chapter is to play one game of "verbal tennis" with Arnett's ideas.

So Here Goes—Serving for the First Point

The concept of "emerging adulthood" has infiltrated the literature not only in the social sciences but also medicine and the arts, and Jeffrey Arnett has been uniquely significant in promoting this terminology and seeing its label being used more and more frequently by researchers in many disciplines. It is still possible to use terminology to describe broad periods of the life course: "childhood," "adolescence," "emerging adulthood," "middle-age," and "old age" can all have a descriptive value in many disciplines as a way of highlighting categories of the life span and focusing on the various implications in understanding individuals' life courses in changing societal conditions. This may be invaluable in focusing on underresearched areas, in illuminating interdisciplinary research, and in guiding policies and professional practices. Hence I concede it has provided a rallying call to researchers across many disciplines.

A Difficult Shot to Counter: Love–Fifteen to You, Jeffrey!

However, a concept and its name do not make a theory, and Arnett's defense against critics such as Bynner (2005) and Côté and Bynner (2008) has lately been to suggest that "There are many emerging adulthoods" (Arnett, 2006a, 2010). This maneuvering to accommodate critical comments rather than offering sound counterarguments seems to me to weaken this so-called theory even further. In an historical analogy, Arnett can be described as the last Spartan stage warrior defending a theoretical castle wall, unaware that over the past decade, and even earlier, systemic theorists have scaled the ramparts in many places, outflanked the defenders and created a new theoretical era, which has allowed a clearer explanation of human development to emerge. Theoretical ideas have moved on since the days of stage theories to accommodate the impact of rapid global and societal changes, which have hugely influenced the varied patterns of youth's transitions to adulthood. Arnett and Tanner have acknowledged this, now accepting that stage theories are redundant and that their ideas refer only to a particular section of the youth population in wealthy Western societies. Despite this, they still cling to the illusion that their descriptions of extended transitions due to young peoples' responses to economic factors, which incidentally are beginning to change again because of the global recession, represent a theory. Moreover, they fall into their own, quite dangerous trap by describing some young people as not being "able to pursue a normal emerging adulthood"—once again making white American middle-class lifestyles the norm and everything else a "deviant" form of transition. Meanwhile Walls and Schafer (2006) have said that "The relevance of a population-average time trend becomes questionable . . . the average may be highly atypical" (p. vi). Hence, structure, dynamics, and development are complex. Factors may have complicated relations to each other, and von Eye and Bogat (2006) state that differences among populations must be explained based on substantive theory!

A Thunderous Volley! I Win This Point: Fifteen–All

To put these remarks above into a more cogent argument, and to attempt to "bring the curtain down" on divergent views between Arnett and Tanner's ideas and ours, I now want to say something about the development of ecological, systemic theories and suggest how they might coexist alongside stage theories. As Waterman (2005) wrote in the *Journal of Adolescence*:

> Over the course of my editorial experiences, I have seen decreasing reference being made to the grand theories of the past, and there is relatively limited new theorizing being developed to replace it . . . Clearly, it is my hope that as the **descriptive findings** [on adolescence] accumulate from both quantitative and qualitative studies, **scholars will seek to do more to incorporate those findings into explanatory systems with potential predictive utility.** Such theories are needed to guide future research, to recommend social policies to promote adolescent welfare and to foster the development of effective intervention strategies for addressing the problems of those adolescents not yet thriving. (pp. 684–685) [My emphases in bold]

This is important, because it is no longer necessary to accept one-variable solutions to research questions or interpret cause and effect from cross-sectional studies. We can now begin to accept the complexities of development and the interactive effects of multilevel variables and seek theoretical frameworks to underpin such empiricism. Bronfenbrenner's (1979) ecological model of human development set the scene for social scientists to consider the interrelationships of forces and factors from a microsocietal to macrosocietal level influencing development, and this was quickly followed by Lerner (1985) and Ford and Lerner (1992), stressing the impact of self-agency and the need for a systemic point of view; Thelen and Smith (1998), who provided empirical evidence for the superiority of systemic approaches over maturational explanations for development, and researchers such as Valsiner (1997) have contributed both theoretically and empirically to these ideas. Even in the context of emerging adulthood, Mitchell's (2006) use of a life course approach to explain transitions to adulthood is more capable of incorporating structural variables, linked lives, self-agency, and the potential of the past to shape the future into a single theory than Arnett's accumulation of minitheories surrounding many different emerging adulthoods.

So to seek explanations as to developmental processes within the various life domains of several subgroups, and individuals, within modern societies, a more sophisticated theoretical framework than Arnett and Tanner's stage model is required, and this is where the challenge of an ecological theory is needed to tease out the multileveled, multifactored, interactive forces and factors involved in human development. As Witherington and Margett (2009, p. 255) wrote, "Perhaps the most vital contribution of the dynamic systems approach is the interpretative framework it provides for all means of analyzing a phenomenon." ·

A Tactical Mistake! Thirty–Fifteen

Arnett is right to some extent—societal changes have created new patterns of the pathways to adulthood, but the varieties and variations of these are responses to global, cultural, and regional shifts, because ecological, social, and economic forces and factors present ever-new and changing challenges to young people growing up in the modern world as they have done for some years now. Clark (2007) has documented how the timing of transitions has changed and been prolonged since the early 1970s among young adults in terms of "the five transitions that many young people make on their way to adulthood: leaving school, leaving their parents' home, having full-year, full-time work, entering conjugal relationships and having children" (2007, p. 13). There has been a decade-by-decade elongation of these transitions, so that Clark found that the typical 25 year old of 2001 had made the same number of transitions as a 22 year old of 1971, whereas a present-day 30 year old has progressed about the same as the 25 year old of the early 1970s, and so on. Thus, the transitions to adulthood have been continually lengthening.

A Fair Point, Jeffrey: Thirty–All!

Côté and Bynner (2008) have presented a cogent argument outlining the deficiencies in Arnett's theoretical position, stating that what he proposes as a new developmental stage is, in fact, responses of the new youth generation to structural changes related to the redistributions of occupations and their effects on transitions from school to work (see also, Heinz, 2007; Hendry & Kloep, 2007a, 2007b). As Westberg (2004) has pointed out previously, various personal or occupational factors, family responsibilities, and particularly parenthood bring individuals to full adult status. So the experiences and processes of making the transition toward adulthood appear to be dependent on whether a prolonged moratorium is the result of choice or social and economic constraints, and whether it is used effectively to gain experiences. Some may acquire skills for adult living and others appear to idle their time away. Within the extended transitions toward adulthood for present-day youths, their responses to the various global and societal shifts play a powerful role in defining the differing pathways young people move along as they mature into early adulthood. Hence, although I am comfortable with broad phases of the life course being called descriptively "childhood," "adulthood," "old age," and so on, explanations and predictions—the life blood of the behavioral sciences—require analyses of the varying processes, mechanisms, and "shifts" that determine the different experiences of individuals as they change and develop across the life span. Only then can we claim interpretation and theory rather than mere description.

For example, Côté and Bynner reason that it is exclusion processes in education and the workplace that prevent young people in certain socioeconomic contexts from experiencing developmental transitions presumed to be advantageous for all emerging adults. They identify various social and economic conditions that over the past few decades have created a prolonged process of progression toward adulthood, arguing that changing economic forces have led to a lowering of the social status of the young and contributed to increasingly precarious trajectories. In turn, these have reduced the social markers associated with the process of individuation (e.g., Beck, 1992). Then the picture becomes more complicated. In drawing attention to the economic, social, and psychological factors that keep some dependent until at least their mid-20s, Côté (2000) earlier concluded that a significant number of young adults have transitional difficulties, and greatest problems come to those with the least economic, intellectual, and psychological resources. Thus, Arnett and Tanner have mistakenly ignored the coping mechanisms of many young people and instead have advanced the view of a deliberately, freely chosen "psychosocial moratorium" that delays entry to adulthood.

A Strategic Error. Forty–Thirty. I'm Now Serving for the Game. . . .

As we have stated throughout the book, the pathways to adult status are more varied and complex than can be described by an essentially descriptive model as offered by Arnett and Tanner. There are a wide range of multilevel, interactive nonlinear, ever-changing forces and factors—globally, culturally, and locally, from within the individual, from the ecological setting, from the existing economic conditions, together with an array of other material and psychosocial influences that would require a dynamic systemic theoretical framework to interpret and explain. Only by linking with such a theoretical perspective could the nuances of different trajectories to adulthood be truly understood. Developmental transitions all across the life span are sufficiently complex to demand a sophisticated, multilayered theoretical model to explain the various processes and mechanisms of change that occur in different ways for different people dependent on cultural, social, ecological, and economic shifts. A developmental stage model must add *explanation* to the developmental process other than amorphous changes over time (e.g., Lerner, 2002). Chronological shift is not sufficient to outline the underlying mechanisms and processes of the transitions to early adulthood. A time–age framework needs to have a more interactive, systemic model incorporated into it to provide the possibility of offering explanation and prediction.

The developing global economic recession has already begun to alter the context of schooling and the social landscape for transitions from adolescence, and fairly recent studies (e.g., Maris et al., 2006; Taylor, 2009) provide evidence that a number of young people are turning to alcohol and drugs to cope with the strains of modern life, and perhaps particularly in relation to transitions from education to an uncertain and precarious labor market, even for those gaining university degrees. Thus, changing social and economic conditions, and other as yet unrecognized factors, into the future may cause even more varied reactions and coping in individuals, and such shifts cannot be predicted by unidimensional, descriptive models.

Pathways to early adulthood have clearly lengthened and become more diverse, but the reasons are because young people have developed a range of coping strategies to meet the challenges of different economic, social, and global shifts, and because there are a myriad of influencing forces and factors, which create many different individual trajectories. But this is not the only problem with Arnett and Tanner's arguments. Both our own and Arnett and Tanner's case studies from Western societies reveal the largely *age-independent* impact of nonnormative shifts, individual experiences, turning points, regression in some life domains, development in others, and psychosocial and material effects on linked lives (Elder & Shanahan, 2006). None of these influences can be exclusively linked to chronological age. On the contrary, they are responsible for accelerating, decelerating, or reversing identity formation. Treating any trajectory that does not completely fit their "mainstream" description of emerging adulthood as an abnormal or exceptional or simply as error variance is a very simplistic way of manipulating the evidence to suit their invented "theory."

Game! I Believe I Win

In conclusion, if we are to accept that the term and concept of "emerging adulthood" provides a terminological focus for researchers from all disciplines, and is a useful general catchphrase for centering descriptions of certain young people in transition within modern affluent societies, I can go along with that. [However, sociologists such as Qvortrup and Christoffersen (1991) might not be too happy with the idea that young people are yet again being described as "human becomings" instead of "human beings"!]. I might concede to calling it a "partial theory"—I have even created some of these myself (for example, the leisure focal theory; Coleman & Hendry, 1990)—but all this strictly within the parameters described and not generalized widely.

To generate ideas, provide predictive strength, and guide policy and practice we have to incorporate some form of systemic model to accommodate the myriad influencing factors and forces that affect young peoples' strivings toward adulthood and to take into consideration the variables that scientists from other disciplines would require to be added to any explanatory equation.

So as I stated at the opening of this section, I always think of tennis when reading something written by Arnett and his colleagues, and now I remember why. The words John McEnroe used to utter at the height of his career when retorting to tennis umpires on close line calls come importantly and relevantly to mind: "You cannot be serious, Man!"

Part IV: Jennifer L. Tanner: It's Not about Winning, It's How You Play the Game

In this play, we the authors have been the players. The audience has been invited to hear two sides of a theoretical debate. Arnett and I have fought to introduce the value in focusing on emerging adults, the lives that they lead, and the new way they come of age in the twenty-first century. Kloep and Hendry dispute the value of this perspective and the theory of emerging adulthood all together. They contend that existing developmental theory and principles override the need for advances in the way we understand the experiences of 18 to 29 year olds. To some extent, this volley of ideas is much ado about nothing—Arnett's theory of emerging adulthood is an articulation of the 18- to 29-year-old experience in the modern, globalizing world. We wholeheartedly embrace the premise that emerging adulthood is a process. Arnett was among the first to ask the question *What is adulthood?*, finding that responses had much more to do with growing and becoming (processes) than being (statuses). And the concept of recentering was an idea I offered (Tanner, 2006) to convey an understanding of emerging adulthood as a process that takes place once and only once in a life span, when the person in context is challenged to dynamically shift in its arrangement of power, control, and responsibility.

In accepting an invitation to debate Kloep and Hendry over the value of the theory of emerging adulthood we did not anticipate fighting a war to defend stage theories. However, we are pleased to have the opportunity to state our belief that the concept of "stage" is the key to developmental science (for more on this issue, see Arnett & Tanner, 2009). At the same time, in response to Kloep and Hendry's call for the use of a systems perspective, we agree. We have embraced developmental systems models and used the framework to elaborate our understanding of development from adolescence, through emerging adulthood, and into young adulthood both in prior work (Arnett & Tanner, 2009; Tanner, 2006) and in this volume (Chapter 2). Our perspective represents an integration of stage and systems theory; we argue for the utility of this approach both in developmental science generally and with regard to emerging adulthood specifically.

Rather than convincing us that "stage" should be eliminated from developmental theory, this debate has strengthened our view that the concept of stages is integral to developmental theory. For us, the integration of stage concepts in developmental systems theory would represent a move forward as a discipline. We embrace the fundamental features of systems theory, but question the lack of focus on the role that power dynamics play in understanding change across the life span development. Family systems theorists accept that power dynamics shift over the course of the family life span. By proxy, power dynamics shift over the course of the individual life span. Most significant is the shift in power that occurs for the individual at the transition to adulthood. Through the process of recentering power, power is transferred from parents to the individual to guide his or her own development in emerging adulthood.

At every stage of development, developmental tasks are supported and facilitated in some subgroups more than in others. Individual and contextual factors, and their interaction, contribute to the unequal distribution of factors that promote optimal outcomes. This is true, also, in emerging adulthood. We see this as the primary source of variation in emerging adult experiences. And we see no reason for this variation to invalidate the distinctiveness of emerging adulthood. In infancy, secure attachment is differentially predictable. Likewise, in emerging adulthood, recentering may be more or less likely, depending on myriad factors that include, but go well beyond, socioeconomic predictors.

Our interactionist view, which embraces the strengths of both stage and systems perspectives, is fundamental to our assertion that emerging adulthood is a developmental stage, but one that is not experienced universally (Arnett, 2006b, 2007b, 2010). We understand emerging adulthood to be a sociocultural adaptation at the individual level. Many if not all life stages have developed historically. Just as "middle childhood" and "adolescence" refer to age groups that are both unique physically, cognitively, and psychologically and distinct in terms of their social roles, so too is emerging adulthood. Thus, we interpret the "emergence" of emerging adulthood in individuals' life spans as an adaptive response to changes at the macrolevels of their ecologies. As the world globalizes, we may be pushed to understand universal development as a function of forces that operate across rather that within cultures. It makes sense that the effects of globalization are seen first in the years during which individuals prepare for the demands of adulthood. We are far from the only theorists to observe that there is a worldwide shift in the goals for training new generations to meet the demands of the new economy. There is widespread talk of the need for "twenty-first century skills," demand for a "creative class," and rise of an "information society." In response, the stage of emerging adulthood provides individuals with an opportunity to take advantage of cognitive gains that can be optimized during these years.

We reject Kloep and Hendry's assertion that the theory of emerging adulthood propagates a Westernized bias of successful development or achievement of adulthood. To the contrary, we take the position that "success" in emerging adulthood must be redefined—moving away from definitions of achievement that include college graduation, marriage, or parenthood as evidence of adjustment. Rather, we contend that making progress through the recentering process defines successful adjustment. This view embraces the developmental process that is emerging adulthood. In constructing the concept of recentering, we have emphasized both developmental process and the role of culture in defining normative development between ages 18 and 29. Within each culture, the developmental history of an individual, the experiences of the individual during emerging adulthood, and the opportunities available play a unique role in defining the pathway that a person will take from adolescence to adulthood. Whether the individual makes progress along that pathway defines success.

In sociology, the majority of work on the transition to adulthood focused and continues to focus on the timing and sequencing of role attainments. By proxy, successful adult development was attained by those who completed their education, married, and became parents in a normative sequence and along a normative timeline. As the life course became individualized, heterogeneity in life paths has been observed in many countries. With increasing entropy, we might expect that the definition of "success" changes, too. Yet the sociological perspective remains tied to the measurement of successful transitions to adulthood as a series of role transitions.

The developmental perspective offers an alternative way of thinking about success during this age period. For example, we expect that taking on role statuses has little to do with successful adaptation. Rather, we contend that both proximal and distal adjustment is better predicted by progress in recentering. That is, we anticipate that resolution of recentering will predict achievement in developmental tasks independent of the role through which goals are obtained [e.g., attaining the right education for one's career goals (rather than a college degree), establishing health and satisfying intimate adult relationships (rather than getting married), and becoming generative in society (through parenting or other roles)].

A substantial number of emerging adults are at risk for failure. Recognizing emerging adulthood as a distinct stage of development that influences pathways between youth and adulthood enhances our understanding of vulnerability and risk, potentially misidentifying targets for resources and policies designed to support emerging adults. For example, vulnerable emerging adults have been primarily identified as those who "age out" of systems that provided services to them as youth: foster care youth, early offenders involved in the juvenile justice system, homeless youth, youth with learning disabilities, and youth with serious mental health problems (Osgood, Foster, Flanagan, & Ruth, 2005). However, this model of identifying vulnerability may mislabel emerging adults in two ways (Tanner, 2007). First, vulnerability in youth does not correspond directly to vulnerability in emerging adulthood. This model tells us little about those who are vulnerable in adolescence and thrive in emerging adulthood. This may be the case when risks associated with youth are eliminated. Second, other systems present risk because individuals do not age out of them. Families often fail youth. The education system also fails youth. These sources represent a double risk—once in youth and once in emerging adulthood—unaccounted for in the vulnerable youth model. Viewing emerging adulthood as a distinct stage of the life span will encourage models that seek to understand how vulnerabilities of youth operate in emerging adulthood and also how emerging adulthood may influence high-risk youth. In turn, efforts to support emerging adult development can be more accurately targeted at those at highest risk for failure.

Because emerging adults tell us that they see themselves as in-between adolescence and adulthood, and because people of all ages acknowledge that becoming adult involves establishing yourself in the adult world with your own identity, based on values and ideas acquired through explorations, we emphasize that emerging adults are engaged in important developmental work during this critical life stage. If we deny the uniqueness of the challenges they face, we may fail to provide them with the scaffolding they need to achieve. Understanding the unique needs of this age group, academic science can play a role in facilitating and optimizing their development and adjustment.

References

Aldwin, C. M. (1992). Aging, coping, and efficacy: Theoretical framework for examining coping in life-span developmental context. In M. L. Wykle & J. Kowal (Eds.), *Stress and health among the elderly* (pp. 96–113). New York: Springer.

Amato, P. R., Booth, A., Johnson, D., & Rogers, S. J. (2007). *Alone together: How marriage in America is changing.* Cambridge, MA: Harvard University Press.

Anderson, R. N., Kochanek, K. D., & Murphy, S. (1997). *Report of final mortality statistics, 1995.* Hyattesville, MD: National Center for Health Statistics.

Aquilino, W. S. (1997). From adolescent to young adult: A prospective study of parent-child relations during the transition to adulthood. *Journal of Marriage and the Family, 59(3),* 670–686.

Aquilino, W. (2006). Family relationships and support systems in emerging adulthood. In J. J. Arnett & J. L. Tanner (Eds.), *Emerging adults in America: Coming of age in the 21st century* (pp. 193–217). Washington, DC: American Psychological Association.

Arias, D. F., & Hernández, A. M. (2007). Emerging adulthood in Spanish and Mexican youth. *Journal of Adolescent Research, 22(5),* 476–503.

Ariès, P. (1962). *Centuries of childhood.* New York: Vintage Books.

Arnett, J. J. (1997). Young people's conceptions of the transition to adulthood. *Youth & Society, 29,* 1–23.

Arnett, J. J. (1998). Learning to stand alone: The contemporary American transition to adulthood in cultural and historical context. *Human Development, 41,* 295–315.

Arnett, J. J. (2000). Emerging adulthood: A theory of development from the late teens through the twenties. *American Psychologist, 55,* 469–480.

Arnett, J. J. (2001). Conceptions of the transition to adulthood: Perspectives from adolescence to midlife. *Journal of Adult Development, 8,* 133–143.

Arnett, J. J. (2003). Conceptions of the transition to adulthood among emerging adults in American ethnic groups. In J. J. Arnett & N. L. Galambos (Eds.), *New directions for child and adolescent development: Cultural conceptions of the transition to adulthood* (No. 100, pp. 63–75). San Francisco: Jossey-Bass.

Arnett, J. J. (2004). *Emerging adulthood: The winding road from late teens through the twenties.* Oxford, UK: Oxford University Press.

Arnett, J. J. (2006a). Emerging adulthood in Europe: A response to Bynner. *Journal of Youth Studies, 9*, 111–123.

Arnett, J. J. (2006b). Emerging adulthood: Understanding the new way of coming of age. In J. J. Arnett, & J. L. Tanner (Eds.), *Emerging adults in America: Coming of age in the 21st century* (pp. 3–20). Washington, DC: American Psychological Association Press.

Arnett, J. J. (2007a). The long and leisurely route: Coming of age in Europe today. *Current History, 106(March)*, 130–136.

Arnett, J. J. (2007b). Suffering, selfish, slackers? Myths and reality about emerging adults. *Journal of Youth and Adolescence, 36*, 23–29.

Arnett, J. J. (2008). The neglected 95%: Why American psychology needs to become less American. *American Psychologist, 63(7)*, 602–614.

Arnett, J. J. (2009). The neglected 95%: A challenge to psychology's philosophy of science. *American Psychologist, 64, 6*, 571–574.

Arnett, J. J. (2011). Emerging adulthood(s): The cultural psychology of a new life stage. In L. A. Jensen (Ed.), *Bridging cultural and developmental psychology: New syntheses in theory, research, and policy* (pp. 255–275). New York: Oxford University Press.

Arnett, J. J., & Hart, A. (2008, August). *Conceptions of adulthood among emerging adults in Denmark and Italy.* Poster presented at the annual meeting of the American Psychological Association, Boston, Massachusetts.

Arnett, J. J., & Taber, S. (1994). Adolescence terminable and interminable: When does adolescence end? *Journal of Youth and Adolescence, 23*, 517–537.

Arnett, J. J., & Tanner, J. L. (Eds.) (2006). *Emerging adults in America: Coming of age in the 21st century* (pp. 3–20). Washington, DC: American Psychological Association Press.

Arnett, J. J., & Tanner, J. L. (2009). Toward a cultural-developmental stage theory of the life course. In K. McCartney & R. Weinberg (Eds.), *Development and experience: A festschrift in honor of Sandra Wood Scarr* (pp. 17–38). New York: Taylor & Francis.

Ataca, B., Kagıtçıbası, C., & Diri, A. (2005). The Turkish family and the value of children: Trends over time. In G. Trommsdorff & B. Nauck (Eds.), *The value of children in cross-cultural perspective: Case studies from eight societies* (pp. 91–119). Lengerich: Pabst Science Publishers.

Atak, H., & çok, F. (2007). Emerging adulthood and perceived adulthood in Turkey. Symposium presented at the 3rd Conference on Emerging Adulthood, Tucson, Arizona, February 15–16.

Avolio, B. J., & Waldman, D. A. (1994). Variations in cognitive, perceptual, and psychomotor abilities, across the working lifespan: Examining the effects of race, sex, experience, education, and occupational type. *Psychology & Aging, 9(3),* 430–442.

Badger, S., Nelson, L. J., & Barry, C. M. (2006). Perceptions of the transition to adulthood among Chinese and American emerging adults. *International Journal of Behavioral Development, 30,* 84–93.

Bagwell, C. L., Bender, S. E., Andreassi, C. L., Kinoshita, T. L., Montarello, S. A., & Muller, J. G. (2005). Friendship quality and perceived relationship changes predict psychosocial adjustment in early adulthood. *Journal of Social and Personal Relationships, 22,* 235–254.

Baltes, P. B. (1987). Theoretical propositions of life-span developmental psychology: On the dynamics between growth and decline. *Developmental Psychology, 23,* 611–626.

Baltes, P. B. (1997). On the incomplete architecture of human ontogeny. Selection, optimization, and compensation as the foundation of developmental theory. *American Psychologist, 52,* 366–380.

Baltes, P.B., Lindenberger, U., & Staudinger, U.M. (2006). Life span theory in developmental psychology. In W. Damon & R.M. Lerner (Eds.), *Handbook of child psychology, Vol. 1* (pp. 569–664). New York: Wiley.

Baltes, P. B., Lindenberger, U., & Staudinger, U. M. (1997). Life-span theory in developmental psychology. In W. Damon & R. M. Lerner (Eds.), *Handbook of child psychology* (5th ed., Vol. 1, pp. 1029–1143). New York: Wiley.

Baltes, P. B., & Staudinger, U. M. (2000). Wisdom: A metaheuristic (pragmatic) to orchestrate mind and virtue toward excellence. *American Psychologist, 55,* 122–136.

Baltes, P. B., Staudinger, U. M., & Lindenberger, U. (1999). Lifespan psychology: Theory and application to intellectual functioning. In L. R. Goldberg et al. (Series Eds.), M. R. Rosenzweig & L. W. Porter (Vol. Eds.), *Annual Review of Psychology* (Vol. 50, pp. 471–507). Palo Alto, CA: Annual Reviews.

Barry, C. M., & Nelson, L. J. (2005). The role of religion in the transition to adulthood for young emerging adults. *Journal of Youth and Adolescence, 34,* 245–255.

Barry, C., Padilla-Walker, L. M., Madsen, S. D., & Nelson, L. J. (2008). The impact of maternal relationship quality on emerging adults' prosocial tendencies: Indirect effects via regulation of pro-social values. *Journal of Youth and Adolescence, 37,* 581–591.

Beck, U. (1992). *Risk society: Towards a new modernity.* London: Sage.

Blinn-Pike, L., Worthy, S. H., Jonkman, J. N., & Smith, G. R. (2008). Emerging adult versus adult status among college students: Examination of explanatory variables. *Adolescence, 43(171),* 577–592.

Bonstein, J. (2008). Zuwanderung: Klares Jein. *Der Spiegel, 30,* 90–91.

Bozick, R. (2007). Making it through the first year of college: The role of students' economic resources, employment, and living arrangements. *Sociology of Education, 80,* 261–285.

Breen, R., & Buchmann, M. (2002). Institutional variation and the position of young people: A comparative perspective. *Annals of the American Academy of Political and Social Science, 580,* 288–305.

Breen, R., & Jonsson, J. O. (2005). Inequality of opportunity in comparative perspective: Recent research on educational attainment and social mobility. *Annual Review of Sociology, 31,* 223–243.

Bronfenbrenner, U. (1979) *The ecology of human development: Experiments by nature and design.* Cambridge, MA: Harvard University Press.

Bronfenbrenner, U., & Morris, P. A. (1998). The ecology of the developmental process. In W. Damon & R. M. Lerner (Eds.), *Handbook of child psychology* (5th ed., Vol. 1, pp. 993–1028). New York: Wiley.

Buchmann, M. (1989). *The script of life in modern society.* Chicago: University of Chicago Press.

Bureau of Labor Statistics. (2005). *Economic news releases: Time Use Survey, 2005.* Washington, DC: Author. Retrieved July 20, 2006, from http://www.bls.gov/tus/.

Bush, B. (2006). *Imperialism and postcolonialism.* London: Longman.

Bynner, J. (2005). Rethinking the youth phase of the life course: The case for emerging adulthood? *Journal of Youth Studies, 8,* 367–384.

Bynner, J. (2008). Transitions to adulthood in a changing world: Consequences for individuals and society from a British perspective. Paper presented at the XI EARA conference in Torino, Italy, May 7–10.

Caldwell, L. (2007). Bravo! Bravo! Bravo!... With a friendly amendment. Open dialogue. *The Psychology of Education Review, 31,* 9–10

Carbery, J., & Buhrmester, D. (1998). Friendship and need fulfillment during three phases of young adulthood. *Journal of Social and Personal Relationships, 15,* 393–409.

Carnethon, M. R., Gidding, S. S., Nehgme, R., Sidney, S., Jacobs, D. R., & Liu, K. (2003). Cardiorespiratory fitness in young adulthood and the development of cardiovascular disease risk factors. *Journal of the American Medical Association, 290,* 3092–3100.

Caspi, A. (1998). Personality development across the life course. In W. Damon & N. Eisenberg (Eds.), *Handbook of child psychology* (5th ed., Vol. 3, pp. 311–338). New York: Wiley.

Castells, M. (1998). *The end of the millennium.* Oxford: Blackwell.

Chang, L. (2008). *Factory girls: From village to city in a changing China.* New York: Spiegel & Grau.

Charles, S. T., Reynolds, C. A., & Gatz, M. (2001). Age-related differences and change in positive and negative affect over 23 years. *Journal of Personality and Social Psychology, 80(1),* 136–151.

Cheah, C. S. L., & Nelson, L. J. (2004). The role of acculturation in the emerging adulthood of aboriginal college students. *International Journal of Behavioural Development, 28,* 495–507.

Chickering, A. W., & Havighurst, R. J. (1981). *The modern American college.* San Francisco: Jossey-Bass.

Child Trends. (last accessed, August 2007). High school dropout rates, accessed at: http://www.childtrendsdatabank.org/indicators/1HighSchoolDropout.cfm and

'Educational Attainment' accessed at http://www.childtrendsdatabank.org/indicat ors/6EducationalAttainment.cfm. Washington, DC: Child Trends.

Clark, W. (2007). Delayed transitions of young adults. *Canadian Social Trends, 84*, Winter, 13–21, accessed at http://www.fedpubs.com/subject/social/cdnsoc.htm.

Coleman, J. C., & Brooks, F. (2009). Key data on adolescence (7th ed.). Brighton, UK: Trust for the Study of Adolescence.

Coleman, J. C., & Hendry, L. B. (1990, 1999). *The nature of adolescence* (3ʳᵈ ed.). London: Routledge.

Coleman, J. C., & Schofield, J. (2007). Key data on adolescence (6th ed.). Brighton, UK: Trust for the Study of Adolescence.

Cook, T., & Furstenberg, F. Jr. (2002). Explaining aspects of the transition to adulthood in Italy, Sweden, Germany and the United States: A cross-disciplinary, case synthesis approach. *Annals of the American Academy of Political and Social Science, 580*, 257–287.

Côté, J. E. (1996). Sociological perspectives on identity formation: The culture-identity link and cultural capital. *Journal of Adolescence, 19*, 417–428.

Côté, J. E. (2000). *Arrested adulthood: The changing nature of identity-maturity in the late-modern world.* New York: NYU Press.

Côté, J. E., & Bynner, J. (2008). Changes in the transition to adulthood in the UK and Canada: The role of structure and agency in emerging adulthood. *Journal of Youth Studies, 11*, 251–268.

Crosnoe, R. (2000). Friendships in childhood and adolescence: The life course and new directions. *Social Psychology Quarterly, 63*, 377–391.

Day, J. C., & Newburger, E. C. (2002). *The big payoff: Educational attainment and synthetic estimates of work-life earnings.* Washington, DC: U.S. Department of Commerce.

Douglass, C. B. (Ed.). (2005). *Barren states: The population "implosion" in Europe.* New York: Berg.

Douglass, C. B. (2007). From duty to desire: Emerging adulthood in Europe and its consequences. *Child Development Perspectives, 1*, 101–108.

Dreher, E. (2007). Optimierung von Selbstwirksamkeit. In A. Bucher, E. Lauermann, & K. Walcher (Eds.), *Ich kann. Du kannst. Wir können. Selbstwirksamkeit und Zutrauen* (pp. 33–58). Wien: Lanz.

Dries-Daffner, I., Hallman, K., Catino, J., & Berdichevsky, K. (2007). Guatemala. In J. J. Arnett (Ed.), *International encyclopedia of adolescence* (Vol. 1, pp. 370–380). New York: Routledge.

Du-Bois Reymond, M. (1998). 'I don't want to commit myself yet': Young people's life concepts. *Journal of Youth Studies, 1*, 63–79.

Elder, G. H. Jr. (1974). *Children of the great depression: Social change in life experience.* Chicago: University of Chicago Press.

Elder, G. H. Jr. (1986). Military times and turning points in men's lives. *Developmental Psychology, 22*, 233–245.

Elder, G. H. Jr. (1987). War mobilization and the life course: A cohort of World War II veterans. *Sociological Forum, 2*, 449–472.

Elder, G. H. Jr. (1997). The life course and human development. In W. Damon & R. M. Lerner (Eds.), *Handbook of child psychology* (4th ed., Vol. 1, pp. 939–991). New York: Wiley.

Elder, G. H. Jr. (1998). The life course as developmental theory. *Child Development, 69* (1), 1–12.

Elder, G. H. Jr., & Shanahan, M. J. (2006). The life course and human development. In W. Damon & R. M. Lerner (Eds.), *Handbook of child psychology* (6th ed., Vol. 1, pp. 665–715). New York: Wiley.

Elnick, A. B., Margrett, J. A., Fitzgerald, J. M., & Labouvie-Vief, G. (1999). Benchmark memories in adulthood: Central domains and predictors of their frequency. *Journal of Adult Development, 6*, 45–59.

Erikson, E. H. (1950). *Childhood and society*. New York: Norton.

Erikson, E. H. (1959). Identity and the life cycle. *Psychological Issues*, Monograph 1. New York: International Universities Press.

Erikson, E. H. (1982). *The life cycle completed*. New York: W.W. Norton.

European Commission. (2007). European social reality. *Special Eurobarometer, 273*. European Commission SOC 98 101387-05E01: Netherlands Family Council.

Evans, K. (2007). Concepts of bounded agency in education, work and the personal lives of young adults. Invited Symposium Paper, 3rd Conference on Emerging Adulthood. Tucson, Arizona, February 15–16.

Facio, A., & Micocci, F. (2003). Emerging adulthood in Argentina. In J. J. Arnett & N. L. Galambos (Eds.), *New directions for child and adolescent development: Cultural conceptions of the transition to adulthood* (No. 100, pp. 21–31). San Francisco: Jossey-Bass.

Facio, A., Resett, S., Micocci, F., & Mistrorigo, C. (2007). Emerging adulthood in Argentina: An age of diversity and possibilities. *Child Development Perspectives, 1*, 115–118.

Fauske, H. (1996). Changing youth: Transition to adulthood in Norway. *Young, 4*, 47–62.

Featherstone, M., & Hepworth, M. (1991). The mask of ageing and the post-modern life course. In M. Featherstone, M. Hepworth, & B. Turner (Eds.), *The body, social process, and cultural theory* (pp. 371–389). London: Sage.

Fergusson, D. M., & Woodward, L. J. (2002). Mental health, educational, and social role outcomes of adolescents with depression. *Archives of General Psychiatry, 59*, 225–231.

Fincham, F. (Ed.) (2010). *Romantic relationships in emerging adulthood*. New York: Cambridge University Press.

Fischer, K. W., & Pruyne, E. (2003). Reflective thinking in adulthood: Emergence, development, and variation. In J. Demick & C. Andreotti (Eds.), *Handbook of adult development* (pp. 169–198). New York: Springer.

Fischer, J. L., Sollie, D. L., Sorell, G. T., & Green, S. K. (1989). Marital status and career stage influences on social networks of young adults. *Journal of Marriage and the Family, 51*, 521–534.

Fischer, K. W., & Bidell, T. R. (1998). Dynamic development of psychological structures in action and thought. In W. Damon & R. M. Lerner (Eds.), *Handbook of child psychology. Vol 1: Theoretical models of human development* (5th ed., pp. 467–561). New York: Wiley.

Fischer, K. W., & Pruyne, E. (2003). Reflective thinking in adulthood: Emergence, development, and variation. In J. Demick & C. Andreotti (Eds.), *Handbook of adult development* (pp. 169–198). New York: Springer.

Fiske, M., & Chiriboga, D. A. (1991). *Change and continuity in adult life*. San Francisco: Jossey Bass.

Flegg, J. L., Morell, C. H., Bos, A. G., Brant, L. J., Talbot, L. A., Wright, J. G., & Lakatta, E. G. (2005). Accelerated longitudinal decline of aerobic capacity in healthy older adults. *Circulation, 112*, 647–682.

Flores, Y. G. (2007). Panama. In J. J. Arnett (Ed.), *International encyclopedia of adolescence* (Vol. 2, pp. 742–750). New York: Routledge.

Ford, D. H., & Lerner, R. M. (1992). *Developmental systems theory: An integrative approach*. New York: Sage.

Freund, A. M., & Baltes, P. B. (2002). Life-management strategies of selection, optimization, and compensation: Measurement by self-report and construct validity. *Journal of Personality & Social Psychology, 82*, 642–662.

Freund, A. M., Li, K. Z. H., & Baltes, P. B. (1999). Successful development and aging: The role of selection, optimization, and compensation. In J. Brandtstädter & R. M. Lerner (Eds.), *Action and self-development: Theory and research through the lifespan* (pp. 401–434). Thousand Oaks, CA: Sage.

Fuligni, A. J. (2007). Family obligation, college enrollment, and emerging adulthood in Asian and Latin American families. *Child Development Perspectives, 1*, 96–100.

Furlong, A., & Cartmel, F. (1997). *Young people and social change: Individualisation and risk in late modernity*. Buckingham: Open University Press.

Fussell, E., & Greene, M. (2002). Demographic trends affecting adolescents around the world. In B. B. Brown, R. Larson, & T. S. Saraswathi (Eds.), *The world's youth: Adolescence in eight regions of the globe* (pp. 21–60). New York: Cambridge University Press.

Fussell, E., Anne H. Gauthier, & Ann Evans. (2007). Heterogeneity in the Transition to Adulthood: The cases of Australia, Canada, and the United States. *European Journal of Population, 23*, 389–414.

Galambos, N., & Martínez, M. L. (2007). Poised for emerging adulthood in Latin America: A pleasure for the privileged. *Child Development Perspectives, 1*, 109–114.

Galambos, N. L., Barker, E. T., & Krahn, H. J. (2006). Depression, self-esteem, and anger in emerging adulthood: Seven-year trajectories. *Developmental Psychology, 42(2)*, 350–365.

Gauthier, A. H. (2007). Becoming a young adult: An international perspective on the transition to adulthood. *European Journal of Population, 23*, 217–223.

Gauthier, A. H., & Furstenberg, F. F. (2002). The transition to adulthood: A time use perspective. *The Annals of the American Academy of Political and Social Sciences, 580*, 153–171.

Giedd, J. N., Blumenthal, J., Jeffries N. O., Castellanos, F. X., Liu, H., Zijdenbos, A., et al. (1999). Brain development during childhood and adolescence: A longitudinal MRI study. *Nature Neuroscience, 2(10)*, 861–863.

Glick, J. E., Ruf, S. D., White, M. J., & Goldscheider, F. (2006). Educational engagement and early family formation: Differences by ethnicity and generation. *Social Forces, 84,* 1391–1415.

Gogtay, N., Giedd, J. N., Lusk, L., Hayashi, K. M., Greenstein, D., Vaituzis, A. C., Nugent, T. F., Herman, D. H., Clasen, L. S., Toga, A. W., Rapoport, J. L., & Thompson, P. M. (2004). Dynamic mapping of human cortical development during childhood through early adulthood. *Proceedings of the National Academy of Sciences, 101(21),* 8174–8179.

Goldscheider, F., & Goldscheider, C. (1994). Leaving and returning home in 20th century America. *Population Bulletin, 48(4),* 2–35.

Goldscheider, F. K., & Goldscheider, C. (1999). Changes in returning home in the US, 1925–1985. *Social Forces, 78,* 695–720.

Gordon-Larsen, P., Nelson, M. C., & Popkin, B. M. (2004). Longitudinal physical activity and sedentary behavior trends: Adolescence to adulthood. *American Journal of Preventive Medicine, 27,* 277–283.

Gottlieb, B. H., Still, E., & Newby-Clark, I. R. (2007). Types and precipitants of growth and decline in emerging adulthood. *Journal of Adolescent Research, 22(2),* 132–155.

Greene, B. (2004). *The fabric of the cosmos.* London, UK: Penguin.

Grob, A., Krings, F., & Bangerter, A. (2001). Life markers in biographical narratives of people from three cohorts: A lifespan perspective in historical context. *Human Development, 44,* 171–190.

Guastello, S. J. (2002). *Managing emergent phenomena. Nonlinear dynamics in work organisations.* Mahwah, NJ: Erlbaum.

Hall, G. S. (1904). *Adolescence: Its psychology, and its relation to physiology, anthropology, sociology, sex, crime, religion and education.* Englewood Cliffs, NJ: Prentice Hall.

Halpern, S. (1998). *The forgotten half revisited: American youth and young families, 1988–2008.* Washington, DC: American Youth Policy Forum.

Hamilton, S., & Hamilton, M. A. (2006). School, work, and emerging adulthood. In J. J. Arnett & J. L. Tanner (Eds.), *Coming of age in the 21st century: The lives and contexts of emerging adults* (pp. 257–277). Washington, DC: American Psychological Association.

Hannum, E., & Jihong, L. (2005). Adolescent transitions to adulthood in reform-era China. In C. Lloyd, J. R. Behrman, N. P. Stromquist, & B. Cohen (Eds.), *The changing transitions to adulthood in developing countries: selected studies* (pp. 270–319). Washington, DC: The National Academy Press.

Hartup, W. W., & Stevens, N. (1999). Friendships and adaptation across the lifespan. *Current Directions in Psychological Science, 8,* 76–79.

Havighurst, R. J. (1972). *Developmental tasks and education* (3rd ed.). New York: McKay.

Heelas, P., Lash, S., & Morris, P. (1996). *Detraditionalization.* London: Wiley-Blackwell.

Heinz, W. R. (1987). The transition from school to work in crisis: Coping with threatening unemployment. *Journal of Adolescent Research, 2*, 127–141.

Heinz, W. R. (2007). *The many faces of emerging adulthood: Social pathways from youth to adulthood*. Paper presented at the 3rd Conference on Emerging Adulthood, Tucson, AZ.

Heinz, W. R. (2009). Youth transitions in an age of uncertainty. In A. Furlong (Ed.), *Handbook of youth and young adulthood* (pp. 3–13). New York: Routledge.

Heinz, W. R., & Marshall, V. W. (Eds.). (2003). *Social dynamics of the life course*. New York: Aldine de Gruyter.

Henderson, S., Holland, J., McGrellis, S., Sharpe, S., & Thomson, R. (2007). *Inventing adulthoods: A biographical approach to youth transitions*. London: Sage.

Hendry, L. B., & Kloep, M. (2002). *Lifespan development: Resources, challenges and risks*. London: Thomson Learning.

Hendry, L. B., & Kloep, M. (2007a). Examining emerging adulthood: Investigating the emperor's new clothes? *Child Development Perspectives, 1(2)*, 74–79.

Hendry, L. B., & Kloep, M. (2007b). Redressing the Emperor: A rejoinder to Jeffrey Arnett. *Child Development Perspectives, 1(2)*, 83–85.

Hendry, L. B., & Kloep, M. (2010). How universal is emerging adulthood? An empirical example. *Journal of Youth Studies, 13(2)*, 169–179.

Hendry, L. B., Shucksmith, J., Love, J., & Glendinning, A. (1993). *Young peoples' leisure and lifestyles*. London: Routledge.

Hershey, D. A., & Farrell, A. H. (1999). Age differences on a procedurally oriented test of practical problem solving. *Journal of Adult Development, 6(2)*, 87–104.

Heuveline, P. (2002). An international comparison of adolescent and young adult mortality. *The Annals of the American Academy of Political and Social Science, 580*, 172–200.

Hofman, M. A. (1997). Lifespan changes in the human hypothalamus. *Experimental Gerontology, 32(4)*, 559–575.

Hofstra, M. B., van der Ende, J., & Verhulst, F. C. (2001). Adolescents' self-reported problems as predictors of psychopathology in adulthood: 10-year follow-up study. *British Journal of Psychiatry, 179*, 203–209.

Holahan, C. J., Valentiner, D. P., & Moos, R. H. (1994). Parental support and psychological adjustment during the transition to young adulthood in a college sample. *Journal of Family Psychology, 8*, 215–223.

Hornblower, M. (1997). Great Xpectations. *Time*, June 9th, pp. 58–68.

Horowitz, A.D., & Bromnick, R.D. (2007). Contestable adulthood: Variability and disparity in markers for negotiating the transition to adulthood. *Youth & Society, 39*, 209–231.

Jensen, A. M. (1994). Feminization of childhood. In J. Qvortrup et al. (Eds.), *Childhood matters. Social theory, practice and politics* (pp. 59–75). Aldershot, UK: Avebury.

Jensen, A. M. (2001). Are the roles of men and women being redefined? Invited paper presented at The Second Demographic Transition in Europe. EuroConference on Family and Fertility Change in Modern European Societies: Explorations and

Explanations of Recent Developments, June 23–28. Bad Herrenalb, Germany. Available at http://www.demogr.mpg.de/Papers/workshops/010623_paper11.pdf.

Jessor, R., Turbin, M. S., & Costa, F. M. (2010). Predicting developmental change in healthy eating and regular exercise among adolescents in China and the United States: The role of psychosocial and behavioural protection and risk. *Journal of Research on Adolescence*, published online May 28.

John, B., & Alwyn, T. (2005). Promoting safe and sensible attitudes to alcohol in children and their families: From lollipops to alcopops. Report to the Alcohol Education Research Council, London, UK.

Jones, G., & Wallace, C. (1992). *Youth, family and citizenship*. Buckingham, UK: Open University Press.

Jones, R. K., Darroch, J. E., & Henshaw, S. K. (2002). Patterns in the socioeconomic characteristics of women obtaining abortions in 2000–2001. *Perspectives on Sexual and Reproductive Health, 34(5)*, 226–235.

Kahneman, D. (2003). Experiences of collaborative research. *American Psychologist, 58*, 723–730.

Kalle, P., Lambrechts, E., & Cuyvers, P. (2000). *Partner interaction*. Partner Interaction, Demography and Equal Opportunities as Future Labour Supply Factors. European Commission SOC 98 101387-05E01. Netherlands Family Council

Kasen, S., Cohen, P., Chen, H., & Castille, D. (2003). Depression in adult women: Age changes and cohort effects. *American Journal of Public Health, 93*, 2061–2066.

Keniston, K. (1965). *The uncommitted: Alienated youth in American society*. New York: Wiley.

Keniston, K. (1971). Youth as a stage of life. In S. D. Feinstein, P. L. Giovacchini, & A. A. Miller (Eds.), *Adolescent psychiatry* (Vol. 1). New York: Aronson.

Kessler, R. C., Berglund, P., Demler, O., Jin, R., & Walters, E. (2005). Lifetime prevalence and age-of-onset distributions of DSM-IV disorders in the National Comorbidity Survey Replication. *Archives of General Psychiatry, 62*, 593–602.

Kessler, R. C., Chiu, W. T., Deler, O., & Walters, E. (2005). Prevalence, severity, and comorbidity of 12-month DSM-IV disorders in the National Comorbidity Survey Replication. *Archives of General Psychiatry, 62*, 617–627.

Kessler, R. C., McGonagle, K. A., Zhao, S., Nelson, C. B., Hughes, M., Eshelman, S., Witchen, H. U., & Kendler, K. S. (1994). Lifetime and 12-month prevalence of DSM-III-R psychiatric disorders in the United States. Results from the National Comorbidity Study. *Archives of General Psychiatry, 51*, 8–19.

Kim-Cohen, J., Caspi, A., Moffitt, T. E., Harrington, H., Milne, B. J., & Poulton, R. (2003). Prior juvenile diagnoses in adults with mental disorder: Developmental follow-back of a prospective-longitudinal cohort. *Archives of General Psychiatry, 60(7)*, 709–717.

Kloep, M. (1999). Love is all you need? Focusing on adolescents' life concerns from an ecological point of view. *Journal of Adolescence, 22*, 49–63.

Kloep, M., & Hendry L. B. (1997). Challenges, risks and coping in adolescence. In D. Messer & S. M. Millar (Eds.), *Exploring developmental psychology: From infancy to adolescence* (pp. 400–416). London: Arnold.

Kloep, M., & Hendry, L. B. (2006). Entry or exit? Transitions into retirement. *Journal of Occupational and Organisational Psychology, 79*, 569–593.

Kloep, M., & Hendry, L. B. (2007). Over-protection, over-protection, over-protection!' Young people in modern Britain. Open dialogue. *The Psychology of Education Review, 31*, 4–7, 18–20.

Kloep, M., & Hendry, L. B. (2008). 'Why should I pay? You've got the means!': Parent-offspring relations in Wales during transitions from adolescence. Paper presented at the 11th Biennal Conference of EARA, Torino, Italy, May 7–10.

Kloep, M., & Hendry, L. B. (2010). Holding on or letting go? *British Journal of Developmental Psychology.* available online: January 13, 2010.

Knafo, A., & Schwartz, S. H. (2009). Accounting for parent-child value congruence: Theoretical considerations and empirical evidence. In U. Schönpflug (Ed.), *Cultural transmission: Psychological, developmental, social, and methodological aspects* (pp. 240–268). New York: Oxford University Press.

Kuate-Defo, B. (2005). Multilevel modeling of influences on transitions to adulthood in developing countries with special reference to Cameroon. In C. Lloyd., J. R. Behrman, N. P. Stromquist, & B. Cohen (Eds.), *The changing transitions to adulthood in developing countries: Selected studies* (pp. 367–423). Washington DC: The National Academy Press.

Labouvie-Vief, G. (1980). Beyond formal operations: Uses and limits of pure logic in life-span development. *Human Development, 23*, 141–160.

Labouvie-Vief, G. (1985). Logic and self-regulation from youth to maturity: A model. In M. Commons, F. Richards, & C. Armon (Eds.), *Beyond formal operations: Late adolescent and adult cognitive development* (pp. 158–180). New York: Praeger.

Labouvie-Vief, G. (2006). Emerging structures of adult thought. In J. J. Arnett & J. L. Tanner (Eds.), *Emerging adults in America: Coming of age in the 21st century* (pp. 193–217). Washington, DC: American Psychological Association.

Labouvie-Vief, G., Chiodo, L. M., Goguen, L. A., Diehl, M., & Orwoll, L. (1995). Representations of self across the lifespan. *Psychology and Aging, 10*, 404–415.

Labouvie-Vief, G., DeVoe, M., & Bulka, D. (1989). Speaking about feelings: Conceptions of emotion across the life-span. *Psychology and Aging, 4*, 425–437.

Labouvie-Vief, G., & Meddler, M. (2002). Affect optimization and affect complexity: Modes and styles of regulation in adulthood. *Psychology and Aging, 10*, 404–415.

Lanz, M., & Tagliabue, S. (2007). Do I really need someone in order to become an adult? Romantic relationship during emergent adulthood in Italy. *Journal of Adolescent Research, 22*, 531–549.

Larson, R. W. (2002). Globalization, societal change, and new technologies: What they mean for the future of adolescence. *Journal of Research on Adolescence, 12(1)*, 1–30.

Larson, R.W., Wilson, S., & Rickman, A. (2010). Globalization, societal change, and adolescence across the world. In R. M. Lerner & L. Steinberg (Eds.), *Handbook of adolescent psychology* (Vol. 2). New York: Wiley.

Lefkowitz, E., & Gillen, M. (2006). Sex is just a normal part of life: Sexuality in emerging adulthood. In J. J. Arnett & J. L. Tanner (Eds.), *Emerging adults in America: Coming of age in the 21st century* (pp. 235–255). Washington, DC: American Psychological Association.

Lerner, R. M. (1984). *On the nature of human plasticity.* New York: Cambridge University Press.

Lerner, R. M. (1985). Adolescent maturational changes and psychosocial development: A dynamic interactional perspective. *Journal of Youth and Adolescence, 14,* 355–372.

Lerner, R. M. (1998). Theories of human development. In W. Damon & R. M. Lerner (Eds.), *Handbook of child psychology* (5th ed., Vol. 1, pp. 1–24). New York: Wiley.

Lerner, R. M. (2002). *Concepts and theories of human development.* Mahwah, NJ: Erlbaum.

Lerner, R.M. (2006). Developmental science, developmental systems, and contemporary theories of human development. In W. Damon & R.M. Lerner (Eds.), *Handbook of child psychology, Vol. 1* (pp. 1-17). New York: Wiley.

Lerner, R. M., Freund, A. M., De Stefanis, I., & Habermas, T. (2001). Understanding developmental regulation in adolescence: The use of the selection, optimization, and compensation model. *Human Development, 44(1),* 29–50.

Levine, M. (2005). *Ready or not, here life comes.* New York: Simon & Schuster.

Levine, P., & Wagner, M. (2005a). Transitions for young adults who received special education services as adolescents: A time of challenge and change. In D. W. Osgood, E. M. Foster, C. Flanagan, & G. R. Ruth (Eds.), *On your own without a net: The transition to adulthood for vulnerable populations* (pp. 202–258). Chicago, IL: The University of Chicago Press.

Levine, P., & Wagner, M. (2005b). Transitional experiences of young adults who received special education services as adolescents: A matter of policy. In D. W. Osgood, E. M. Foster, C. Flanagan, & G. R. Ruth (Eds.), *On your own without a net: The transition to adulthood for vulnerable populations* (pp. 259–271). Chicago, IL: The University of Chicago Press.

Levinson, D. J., with Darrow, C. N., Klein, E. B., Levinson, M. H., & McKee, B. (1978). *The seasons of a man's life.* New York: Knopf.

Lewis, M. (1997). Personality self-organization: Cascading constraints on cognition-emotion interactions. In A. Fogel, M. C. D.P. Lyra, & J.Valsiner (Eds.), *Dynamics and indeterminism in developmental and social processes* (pp. 193–216). Mahwah, NJ: Lawrence Erlbaum Associates, Inc.

Lewis, M. D. (2000). The promise of dynamic systems approaches for an integrated account of human development. *Child Development, 71,* 36–43.

Lewis, S. K., Ross, C. E., & Mirowsky, J. (1999). Establishing a sense of personal control in the transition to adulthood. *Social Forces, 77(4),* 1573–1599.

Lloyd, C. (Ed.) (2005). *Growing up global: The changing transitions to adulthood in developing countries.* Washington, DC: National Research Council and Institute of Medicine. New York: National Academies Press.

Lloyd, C. B., Behrman, J. R., Stromquist, N. P., & Cohen, B. (Eds.). (2005). *The changing transitions to adulthood in developing countries: Selected studies.* Washington, DC: The National Academy Press.

Loevinger, J. (1976). *Ego development: Conceptions and theories.* San Francisco: Jossey-Bass.

Luyckx, K., Schwartz, S. J., Goossens, L., & Pollochl, S. (2008). Employment, sense of coherence, and identity formation. *Journal of Adolescent Research, 23(5),* 566–591.

Macek, P., Bejček, J., & Vaníčková, J. (2007). Contemporary Czech emerging adults: Generation growing up in the period of social changes. *Journal of Adolescent Research, 22,* 444–475.

Machado Pais, J. (2002). Laberintos de vida: Paro juvenil y rutas de salida (jóvenes portugueses). *Revista de Estudios de Juventud, 56,* 87–101.

Maris, P., Brosnan, M., Faulkner, N., & Vital, P. (2006). 'They are out of control': Self perceptions, risk-taking and attributional styles of adolescents with SEDB's. *Emotional and Behavioural Difficulties, 11(4),* 281–298.

Martín, M. (2002). La prolongación de la etapa juvenil de la vida y sus efectos en la socialización. *Revista de Estudios de Juventud, 56,* 103–118.

Masten, A. S., Burt, K., Roisman, G. I., Obradovic, J., Long, J. D., & Tellegen, A. (2004). Resources and resilience in the transition to adulthood: Continuity and change. *Development and Psychopathology, 16,* 1071–1094.

Masten, A. S., Obradovic, J., & Burt, K. B. (2006). Resilience in emerging adulthood: Developmental perspectives on continuity and transformation. In J. J. Arnett & J. L. Tanner (Eds.), *Emerging adults in America: Coming of age in the 21st century* (pp. 193–217). Washington, DC: American Psychological Association.

Mathews, T. J., & Hamilton, B. E. (2009). Delayed childbearing: More women are having their first child later in life. *NCHS Data Brief, 21,* 1–8.

Mayseless, O., & Scharf, M. (2003). What does it mean to be an adult? The Israeli experience. *New Directions in Child and Adolescent Development, 100,* 5–20.

McTigue, K. M., Garrett, J. M., & Popkin, B. M. (2002). The natural history of the development of obesity in a cohort of young US adults, 1981–1998. *Annals of Internal Medicine, 136(12),* 857–864.

Merluzzi, T. V., & Nairn, R. C. (1999). Adulthood and aging: Transitions in health and health cognition. In T. L. Whitman, T. V. Merluzzi, & R. D. White (Eds.), *Life-span perspectives on health and illness* (pp. 189–206). Mahwah, NJ: Erlbaum.

Milevsky, A. (2005). Compensatory patterns of sibling support in emerging adulthood: Variations in loneliness, self-esteem, depression, and life satisfaction. *Journal of Social and Personal Relationships, 22,* 743–755.

Mirowsky, J., & Ross, C. E. (1999). Economic hardship across the life course. *American Sociological Review, 64(4),* 548–569.

Mitchell, B. (2004). Making the move: Cultural and parental influences on Canadian young adults' home-leaving decisions. *Journal of Comparative Family Studies, 35,* 423–441.

Mitchell, B. A. (2006). Changing courses: The pendulum of family transitions in comparative perspective. *Journal of Comparative Family Studies, 37,* 325–343.

Mollenkopf, J., Waters, M. C., Holdaway, J., & Kasinitz, P. (2005). The ever-winding path: Ethnic and racial diversity in the transition to adulthood. In R.A. Settersten,

Jr., F.F. Furstenberg, Jr., & R.G. Rumbaut (Eds.), *On the frontier of adulthood: Theory, research, and public policy* (pp. 454–497). Chicago: University of Chicago Press.

Montgomery, M. J. (2005). Psychosocial intimacy and identity: From early adolescence to emerging adulthood. *Journal of Adolescent Research, 20*, 346–374.

Montgomery, M. J., & Sorell, G. T. (1994). Differences in love attitudes across family life stages. *Family Relations, 46*, 55–61.

National Center for Education Statistics. (2009). *The condition of education, 2009*. Washington, DC: U.S. Department of Education. Available at <www.nces.gov>.

National Center for Education Statistics. (2010). *The condition of education, 2010*. Washington, DC: U.S. Department of Education. Available at <www.nces.gov>.

National Center for Health Statistics. (2005). *Health, United States, 2005 with chartbook on trends in the kealth of Americans*. Hyattsville, MD.

Nelson, L. J. (2009). An examination of emerging adulthood among Romanian college students. *International Journal of Behavioral Development, 33*, 402–411.

Nelson, L. J., Badger, S., & Wu, B. (2004). The influence of culture in emerging adulthood: Perspectives of Chinese college students. *International Journal of Behavioral Development, 28*, 26–36.

Nelson, L. J., & Chen, X. (2007). Emerging adulthood in China: The role of social and cultural factors. *Child Development Perspectives, 1*, 86–91.

Nelson, L. J., & McNamara Barry, C. (2005). Distinguishing features of emerging adulthood: The role of self-classification as an adult. *Journal of Adolescence Research, 20*, 242–262.

Newman, M. (2008). Massive shift leaves students adrift and tutors 'swamped.' *Times Higher Education, 851(1)*, 17–23.

Nurmi, J-E. (1993). Adolescent development in an age-graded context: The role of personal beliefs, goals, and strategies in the tackling of developmental tasks and standards. *International Journal of Behavioral Development, 16*, 169–189.

Nurmi, J-E. (1997). Self-definition and mental health during adolescence and young adulthood. In J. Schulenberg, J. L. Maggs, & K. Hurrelman (Eds.), *Health risks and developmental transitions during adolescence* (pp. 395–419). New York: Cambridge University Press.

Nurmi, J-E., & Salmelo-Aro, K. (2002). Goal construction, reconstruction and depressive symptoms in a life-span context: The transition from school to work. *Journal of Personality, 70(3)*, 385–420.

O'Donnell, K. (2006). Adult education participation in 2004–2005. National Center for Education Statistics. Accessed online at http://nces.ed.gov.

OECD (1998). *Work force aging in OECD countries. OECD employment outlook* (Chapter 4, pp. 123–150). Paris, France: OECD Publishing.

OECD (2009). *Society at a glance, 2009*. Geneva, Switzerland: Author.

Osgood, D. W., Foster, E. M., Flanagan, C., & Ruth, G. R. (Eds.). (2005). *On your own without a net: The transition to adulthood for vulnerable populations*. Chicago, IL: University of Chicago Press.

Papastefanou, C. (1999). Adult daughters' relationship with their parents and their leaving home in three different countries. Paper presented at the 9th European Conference on Developmental Psychology, September 1–5. Spetses, Greece.

Paradis, A. D., Reinherz, H. Z., Giaconia, R. M., & Fitzmaurice, G. (2006). Major depression in the transition to adulthood: The impact of active and past depression on young adult functioning. *The Journal of Nervous and Mental Disease, 194,* 318–323.

Parker, H., Aldridge, J., & Measham, F. (1998). *Illegal leisure.* London, UK: Routledge.

Peck, S. C., Vida, M., & Eccles, J. S. (2008). Adolescent pathways to adulthood drinking: Sport activity involvement is not necessarily risky or protective. *Addiction, 103,* 69–83.

Perna, L. W. (2003). The private benefits of higher education: An examination of the earnings premium. *Research in Higher Education, 44(3),* 451–472.

Perry, W. G. Jr. (1970). *Forms of intellectual and ethical development in the college years.* New York: Holt, Rinehart, & Winston.

Perry, W. G. Jr. (1981). Cognitive and ethical growth. In A. Chickering (Ed.), *The modern American college* (pp. 76–116). San Francisco: Jossey-Bass.

Pinker, S. (1995). Language acquisition. In L. Gleitman & M. Liberman (Eds.), *An invitation to cognitive science* (2nd ed., Vol. 1: *Language,* pp. 135–182). Cambridge, MA: MIT Press.

Pulakos, J. (2001). Young adult relationships: Siblings and friends. *Journal of Psychology, 123,* 237–244.

Quisumbing, A. R, & Hallman, K. (2005). Marriage in transition: Evidence on age, education, and assets from six developing countries. In C. Lloyd, J. P. Behrman, N. P. Stromquist, & B. Cohen (Eds.), *The changing transitions to adulthood in developing countries: selected studies* (pp. 200–269). Washington DC: The National Academy Press.

Qvortrup, J., & Christoffersen, M. N. (1991). *Childhood as a social phenomenon.* Vienna, Austria. European Centre.

Regan, P. C., Durvasula, R., Howell, L., Ureño, O., & Rea, M. (2004). Gender, ethnicity, and the developmental timing of first sexual and romantic experiences. *Social Behavior and Personality, 32,* 667–676.

Reifman, A., Arnett, J. J., & Colwell, M. J. (2006). Emerging adulthood: Theory, assessment, and application. *Journal of Youth Development, 1,* 1–12.

Reitzle, M. (2006). The connections between adulthood transitions and the self-perception of being adult in the changing contexts of East and West Germany. *European Psychologist, 11,* 26–38.

Riegel, K. F. (1975). Toward a dialectical theory of development. *Human Development, 18,* 50–64.

Riegel, K. F. (1979). *Foundations of dialectical psychology.* New York: Academic Press.

Robbins, A., & Wilner, A. (2001). *Quarterlife crisis: The unique challenges of life in your twenties.* New York: Tarcher/Putnam.

Roberts, B. W., Caspi, A., & Moffitt, T. E. (2001). The kids are alright: Growth and stability in personality development from adolescence to adulthood. *Journal of Personality and Social Psychology, 81(4),* 670–683.

Roberts, B. W., Caspi, A., & Moffitt, T. E. (2003). Work experiences and personality development in young adulthood. *Journal of Personality and Social Psychology, 84(3),* 582–593.

Roberts, B. W., O'Donnell, M., & Robins, R. W. (2004). Goal and personality trait development in emerging adulthood. *Journal of Personality and Social Psychology, 87,* 541–550.

Roberts, B. W., Walton, K. E., & Viechtbauer, W. (2006). Patterns of mean-level change in personality traits across the life course: A meta-analysis of longitudinal studies. *Psychological Bulletin, 132(1),* 1–25.

Roberts, C. M. (2009). *An in-depth appraisal of transitional experiences in professional cricket.* Unpublished Doctoral Thesis, University of Glamorgan.

Roberts, K., & Parsell, G. (1994). Youth cultures in Britain: The middle class take-over. *Leisure Studies, 13,* 33–48.

Robins, L. N., & Regier, D. A. (1991). *Psychiatric disorders in America: The Epidemiological Catchment Area Study.* New York: The Free Press.

Robins, R. W., Fraley, R. C., Roberts, B. W., & Trzesniewski, K. H. (2001). A longitudinal study of personality change in young adulthood. *Journal of Personality, 69(4),* 617–640.

Robinson, L. C. (2000). Interpersonal relationship quality in young adulthood: A gender analysis. *Adolescence, 35,* 775–784.

Roest, A. M. C., Dubas, J. S., & Gerris, J. R. M. (2009). Value transmissions between fathers, mothers, and adolescent and emerging adult children: The role of the family climate. *Journal of Family Psychology, 23,* 146–155.

Roisman, G. I., Masten, A. S., Coatsworth, J. D., & Tellegen, A. (2004). Salient and emerging developmental tasks in the transition to adulthood. *Child Development, 75,* 123–133.

Rönkä, A., Oravala, S., & Pulkkinen, L. (2003). Turning points in adults' lives: The effects of gender and the amount of choice. *Journal of Adult Development, 10(3),* 203–215.

Rosenbaum, J. E. (2002). *Beyond empty promises: Policies to improve transitions into college and jobs.* (Contract No. ED99CO0160) Washington DC: Office of Vocational and Adult Education, U.S. Department of Education.

Rosenbaum, J. E., & Person, A. E. (2003). Beyond college for all: Policies and practices to improve transitions into college and jobs. *Professional School Counseling, 6,* 252–259.

Rosenberger, N. (2007). Rethinking emerging adulthood in Japan: Perspectives from long-term single women. *Child Development Perspectives, 1,* 92–95.

Rusconi, A. (2004). Different pathways out of the parental home: A comparison of West Germany and Italy. *Journal of Comparative Family Studies, 35(4),* 627–649.

Rutter, M. (1996). Psychological adversity: Risk, resilience and recovery. In L. Verhofstadt-Deneve, I. Kienhorst, & C. Braet (Eds.), *Conflict and development in adolescence* (pp. 21–34). Leiden, The Netherlands: DSWO Press.

Salter, R. B. (1998). *Textbook of disorders and injuries of the musculoskeletal system* (3rd ed.). Philadelphia PA: Lippincott Williams & Wilkins.

Samter, W. (2003). Friendship interaction skills across the lifespan. In J. O. Greene & B. R. Burleson (Eds.), *Handbook of communication and social interaction skills* (pp. 637–684). Mahwah, NJ: Erlbaum.

Sassler, S. (2004). The process of entering into cohabitating unions. *Journal of Marriage and Family, 66,* 491–505.

Scabini, E., & Marta, E. (2006). Changing intergenerational relationship. *European Review, 14,* 81–98.

Scabini, E., Marta, E., & Lanz, M. (2006). *The transition to adulthood and family relations: An intergenerational perspective.* London: Psychology Press.

Schaefer, R. T. (2006). *Racial and ethnic groups.* Upper Saddle River, NJ: Prentice Hall.

Schaie, K. W. (1977). Toward a stage theory of adult cognitive development. *International Journal of Aging and Human Development, 8,* 129–138.

Schaie, K. W. (1983). What can we learn from the longitudinal study of adult development? In K. W. Schaie (Ed.), *Longitudinal studies of adult psychological development* (pp. 1–19). New York: Guilford Press.

Schlegel, A., & Barry, H. (1991). *Adolescence: An anthropological inquiry.* New York: Free Press.

Schnaiberg, A., & Goldenberg, S. (1989). From empty nest to crowded nest: The dynamics of incompletely-launched young adults. *Social Problems, 36,* 251–269.

Schoeni, Robert F., and Karen Ross. 2005. "Material Assistance from Families during the Transition to Adulthood." In *On the Frontier of Adulthood: Theory, Research, and Public Policy* edited by Settersten, Richard A. Jr.; Furstenberg, Frank F. Jr.; Rumbaut, Rubén G. Chicago: University of Chicago Press.

Schooler, C., Mulatu, M. S., & Oates, G. (2004). Occupational self-direction, intellectual functioning, and self-directed orientation in older workers: Findings and implications for individuals & societies. *American Journal of Sociology, 110,* 161–197.

Schoon, I. (2006). *Risk and resilience: Adaptations in changing times.* Cambridge, UK: Cambridge University Press.

Shucksmith, J., & Hendry, L. B. (1998). *Health issues and adolescents: Growing up, speaking out.* London & New York: Routledge.

Schulenberg, J. E., O'Malley, P. M., Bachman, J. G., & Johnston, L. D. (2000). "Spread your wings and fly": The course of well-being and substance use during the transition to young adulthood. In L. J. Crockett & R. K. Silbereisen (Eds.), *Negotiating adolescence in times of social change* (pp. 224–255). New York: Cambridge University Press.

Schulenberg, J. E., & Zarrett, N. R. (2006). Mental health during emerging adulthood: Continuity and discontinuity in courses, causes, and functions. In J. J. Arnett &

J. L. Tanner (Eds.), *Emerging adults in America: Coming of age in the 21st century* (pp. 193–217). Washington, DC: American Psychological Association.

Schuman, H., & Scott, J. (1989). Generations and collective memories. *American Sociological Review, 54,* 359–381.

Schwartz, S. J., Côté, J., & Arnett, J. J. (2005). Identity and agency in emerging adulthood: Two developmental routes in the individualization process. *Youth & Society, 37(2),* 201–229.

Seiffge-Krenke, I. (2003). Testing theories of romantic development from adolescence to young adulthood: Evidence of a developmental sequence. *International Journal of Behavioral Development, 27,* 519–531.

Seiffge-Krenke, I. (2007). Leaving home or still in the nest? Parent-child relationships and psychological health as predictors of different leaving home patterns. *Developmental Psychology, 42(5),* 864–876.

Seiffge-Krenke, I., & Gelhaar, T. (2008). Does successful attainment of developmental tasks lead to happiness and success in later developmental tasks? A test of Havighurst's (1948) theses. *Journal of Adolescence, 31,* 33–52.

Settersten, R. A., Furstenberg, F. F., & Rumbaut, R. G. (2005). *On the frontier of adulthood: Theory, research and public policy.* Chicago: University of Chicago Press.

Sheehy, G. (1976). *Passages.* New York: E. P. Dutton.

Shixun, G. (1994). A pattern study: China's family of the elderly and community care in the future. In The Hongkong Council of Social Services (Ed.), *Conference Proceedings of the International Conference on Family and Community Care* (pp. 168–172). Hong Kong, China.

Shucksmith, J., & Hendry, L. B. (1998). *Health issues and adolescents: Growing up, speaking out.* London & New York: Routledge.

Shucksmith, J., Hendry, L. B., & Glendinning, A. (1995). Models of parenting: Implications for adolescent well-being within different types of family contexts. *Journal of Adolescence, 18,* 253–270.

Shulman, N. (1975). Life-cycle variations in patterns of close relationships. *Journal of Marriage and the Family, 37,* 813–821.

Shulman, S., Scharf, M., Lumer, D., & Maurer, O. (2001). Parental divorce and young adult children's romantic relationships: Resolution of the divorce experience. *American Journal of Orthopsychiatry, 71,* 473–478.

Shweder, R. A., Goodnow, J., Hatano, G., Levine, R. A., Markus, H., & Miller, P. (2006). The cultural psychology of development: One mind, many mentalities. In W. Damon (Ed.), *Handbook of child development* (5th ed., Vol. 1, pp. 865–937) New York: Wiley.

Small, S., & Supple, A. (2001). Communities as system: Is a community more than the sum of its parts? In A. Booth & A. C. Crouter (Eds.), *Does it take a village? Community effects on children, adolescents and families* (pp. 161–174). Mahwah, NJ: Erlbaum.

Smeeding, T. (2005). Public policy, economic inequality, and poverty: The United States in comparative perspective. *Social Science Quarterly, 86,* 956–983.

Smith, J., Staudinger, U. M., & Baltes, P. B. (1994). Occupational settings facilitating wisdom-related knowledge. *Consulting and Clinical Psychology, 62,* 986–999.

Smock, Pamela, and Fiona Rose Greenland. 2010. "Diversity in pathways to parenthood: Patterns, implications, and emerging research directions." *Journal of Marriage and Family,* 72(3): 576–593.

Sorell, G. T., SoRelle-Miner, D., & Pause, C. J. (2007). Moving on: The challenges of dynamic systems perspective. *Human Development, 50,* 160–164.

Sowell, E. R., Peterson, B. S., Thompson, P. M., Welcome, S. E., Henkenius, A. L., & Toga, A. W. (2003). Mapping cortical change across the human life span. *Nature Neuroscience, 6,* 309–315.

Sowell, E. R., Thompson, P. M., & Toga, A. W. (2004). Mapping changes in the human cortex throughout the span of life. *The Neuroscientist, 10(4),* 372–392.

Spencer, J. P., Clearfield, M., Corbetta, D., Ulrich, B., Buchanan, P., & Schöner, G. (2006). Moving toward a grand theory of development: In Memory of Esther Thelen. *Child Development, 77(6),* 1521–1538.

Sprecher, S., & Felmlee, D. (1992). The influence of parents and friends on the quality and stability of romantic relationships: A three-wave longitudinal investigation. *Journal of Marriage and the Family, 54(4),* 888–900.

Sternberg, R. J., Forsythe, G. B., Hedlund, J. Horvorth, J. A., Wagner, R. K., Williams, W. M. et al. (2000). *Practical intelligence in everyday life.* Cambridge, UK: Cambridge University Press.

Sternberg, R. J., & Grigorenko, E. L. (Eds.). (2002). *The general factor of intelligence: How general is it?* Mahwah, NJ: Erlbaum.

Stewart, I., & Vaitlingham, R. (Eds.). (2004). *Seven ages of man and woman: A look at Britain in the second Elizabethan era.* Swindon, UK: ESRC.

Swartz, T. T., & O'Brien, K. B. (2009). Intergenerational support during the transition to adulthood. In A. Furlong (Ed.), *Handbook of youth and young adulthood* (pp. 3–13). New York: Routledge.

Tammelin, T., Laitinen, J., & Näyhä, S. (2004). Change in the level of physical activity from adolescence into adulthood and obesity at the age of 31 years. *International Journal of Obesity, 28,* 775–782.

Tanner, J. L. (2006). Recentering during emerging adulthood. In J. J. Arnett & J. L. Tanner (Eds.), *Emerging adults in America: Coming of age in the 21st century* (pp. 193–217). Washington, DC: American Psychological Association.

Tanner, J. L. (2007). Book review: On your own without a net: The transition to adulthood for vulnerable populations. *Social Service Review, 81(1),* 186–191.

Tanner, J. L., Reinherz, H. Z., Beardslee, W. R., Fitzmaurice, G. M., Leis, J. A., & Berger, S. R. (2007). Change in prevalence of psychiatric disorders from 21 to 30 in a community sample. *Journal of Nervous and Mental Disease, 195(4),* 298–306.

Taylor, P. (2009). Stress and coping strategies in teenagers facing examinations. Paper presented at the British Psychological Society's Division of Educational and Child Psychology, Manchester, UK, January 7–9.

Thelen, E., & Bates, E. A. (2003). Connectionism and dynamic systems: Are they really different? *Developmental Science, 6,* 378–391.

Thelen, E., & Smith, L. B. (1998). *A dynamic systems approach to the development of cognition and action* (3rd ed.) Cambridge, MA: MIT Press.

Thelen, E., & Smith, L. B. (2006). Dynamic systems theories. In W. Damon & R. M. Lerner (Eds.), *Handbook of child psychology* (6th ed., Vol. 1, pp. 258–312). New York: Wiley.

Thomson, R., & Holland, J. (2002). Imagining adulthood: Resources, plans and contradictions. *Gender and Education, 14(4),* 337–350.

Thornton, S. (2008). *Understanding human development.* Basingstoke, UK: Palgrave Macmillan.

Twenge, J. M. (2006). *Generation me: Why today's young Americans are more confident, assertive, entitled—and more miserable than ever before.* New York: Free Press.

U. S. Department of Health and Human Services. (2000). *Healthy people 2010.* Washington, DC: U.S. Department of Health and Human Services.

UNICEF. (2003). *The state of the world's children.* Oxford, UK: Oxford University Press.

Vaillant, G. E. (2002). *Aging well.* New York: Little Brown.

Valsiner, J. (1997). *Culture and the development of children's action: A theory of human development* (2nd ed.). New York: Wiley.

Veblen, T. (1899, reprinted 2008). *The theory of the leisure class.* Oxford, UK: Oxford University Press.

Von Eye, A. & Bogat, G.A. (2006). Person-oriented and variable-oriented research. *Merrill Palmer Quarterly, 53,* 390–420.

Vygotsky, L. S. (1930). Tool and symbol in children's development. In M. Cole, V. John-Steiner, S. Scribner, & E. Souberman (Eds.), *L. S. Vygotsky: Mind in society,* Cambridge, MA: Harvard University Press,

Walls, T. A., & Schafer, J. L. (Eds.) (2006). *Models for intensive longitudinal data.* Oxford, UK: Oxford University Press

Walther, A. (2009). "It was not my choice, you know!" Young people's subjective views and decision-making processes in biographical transitions. In I. Schoon & R.K. Silbereisen (Eds.), *Transitions from school to work: Globalization, individualization, and patterns of diversity* (pp. 121–144). New York: Cambridge University Press.

Waterman, A. (2005). Reflections on changes in research on adolescence from the perspective of fifteen years of editorial experiences. *Journal of Adolescence, 28,* 681–685.

Webster, G., & Goodwin, B. C. (1996). *Form and transformation: Generative and relational principles in biology.* Cambridge, UK: Cambridge University Press.

Weisner, T., & Lowe, D. E. (2005). Globalization, childhood, and psychological anthropology. In C. Casey & R. B. Edgerton (Eds.), *A companion to psychological anthropology: Modernity and psychocultural change* (pp. 315–336). London, UK: Wiley-Blackwell.

Westberg, A. (2004). Forever young? Young people's conception of adulthood: The Swedish case. *Journal of Youth Studies, 7(1),* 35–53.

Westenberg, P. M., & Gjerde, P. F. (1999). Ego development during the transition from adolescence to young adulthood: A 9-year longitudinal study. *Journal of Research in Personality, 33(2)*, 233–252.

Whitbourne, S. K. (1986). *The me I know: A study of adult identity*. New York: Springer-Verlag.

Whiting, B. B. (1998). The meaning of independence and responsibility. *Human Development, 41*, 321–322.

William T. Grant Foundation Commission on Work, Family, and Citizenship. (1988). *The forgotten half: Non-college youth in America*. Washington, DC: Author.

William T. Grant Foundation, Halperin, S. (Ed.). (1998). *The forgotten half revisited*. Washington, DC: American Youth Policy Forum.

Winsborough, H. H. (1978). Statistical histories of the life circle of birth cohorts: The transition from schoolboy to adult male. In K. E. Teuber, K. E. Bumpass, & J. A. Sweet (Eds.), *Social demography* (pp. 231–259). New York: Academic Press.

Witherington, D. C. (2007). The dynamic systems approach as metatheory for developmental psychology. *Human Development, 50*, 127–153.

Witherington, D. C. & Margett, T. E. (2009) Systems and dynamic systems: the search for inclusive merger. *Human Development, 52*, 251–256.

Wittchen, H., Nelson, C. B., & Lachner, G. (1998). Prevalence of mental disorders and psychosocial impairments in adolescence and young adults. *Psychological Medicine, 28*, 109–126.

Wolbers, M.H. J. (2007). Patterns of labor market entry: A comparative perspective on school to work transitions in 11 European countries. *Acta Sociologica, 50*, 189–210.

World Health Organisation. (2008). WHO Statistical Information System (WHOSIS), available online at http://www.who.int/whosis/en/ (last accessed June 2008).

Yates, J. A. (2005). The transition from school to work: Education and work experiences. *Monthly Labor Review, 128(2)*, 21–32.

Zentner, M., & Renaud, M. (2007). Origins of adolescents' ideal self: An intergenerational perspective. *Journal of Personality and Social Psychology, 92*, 557–574.

Index

Printed in the USA/Agawam, MA
February 12, 2014

585173.070